JOY OF READING

JOY OF READING

One family's fun-filled guide to reading success

by Debbie Duncan

Also by Debbie Duncan

When Molly Was in the Hospital: A Book for Brothers and Sisters of Hospitalized Children

Cover Design: Royal Windsor Graphics
Book Design: Serena Standley

Rayve Productions Inc.
Box 726 Windsor CA 95492 USA

Text copyright © 1998 Debbie Duncan

Printed in the United States of America

Publisher's Cataloging in Publication
Duncan, Debbie
   Joy of Reading: one family's fun-filled guide to reading success / by Debbie Duncan
      p.   cm.
   Includes index.
   ISBN 1-877810-45-2 (alk. paper)

   1. Children--United States--Books and reading.   2. Children's literature--Bibliography.
   3. Children's fiction--Bibliography.

   I. Title.

Z1037.D84   1997
[PN 1009.A1]
028.1'62--dc21   97-35073
                                                                             CIP

For my mother and father,
Lavon and Don Duncan,
who first introduced me to the joy of reading

Contents

Acknowledgments

This book is a labor of love. Bill, Jennifer, Allison, and Molly know that as my family they are both my inspiration and my salvation. My writers group — Cynthia Chin-Lee, Nancy Farmer, Cherry Lyon Jones, SuAnn and Kevin Kiser, Nina Ollikainen, Peggy Rathmann, Rita Seymour, and Mary Elizabeth Wildberger — gave me encouragement as well as editorial advice and friendship. I am also grateful to fellow writers Debra Keller and Karen Romano Young, my e-mail buddies who read the entire manuscript and, like the writers group that meets in my dining room, believe I have something valuable to say about children's books.

Many friends were eager to share stories about their family's favorite books. Catherine Jordan and Terrie Gordon-Gamble, in particular, gave me enough material for entire chapters. They have my gratitude, as do my other friends from whom I gleaned information. I'd also like to thank my daughters' friends who cheerfully talked with me about books that lived on for them beyond the final page.

Librarians and children's bookstore staff members were always willing to help me find the information I needed, or just to stop and chat about great books. I'm especially grateful to Katy Obringer and Maya Spector of Palo Alto Children's Library and Alice Bethke, formerly of Palo Alto Unified School District, and Linda and Dennis Ronberg and their staff at Linden Tree Children's Records and Books in

Los Altos. All parents should be so fortunate to have such uncommon resources in their community.

I also want to thank KGO radio talk-show host Ronn Owens and his producer, Patty Stanton, for giving me the opportunity to share my thoughts, experiences, and enthusiasm about reading and children's books with the San Francisco Bay Area. It's always a treat.

Finally, I consider myself one of the luckiest authors in America to be working with Barbara and Norm Ray, publishers who believe in literacy and literature, and children and families. *Joy of Reading* was their idea. It has been my pleasure to write it.

Part One

Books Through the Years

Who Am I and Why Am I Writing This Book?

When I was expecting my first child thirteen years ago, I frequently daydreamed about what kind of parent I would be. I'm not talking about "quality," because of course I assumed I would be a good parent (doesn't everyone?). No, I mean what "type" of parent. Would I be a birthday party mom? a park parent? a little league supporter? one who frequents museums? or maybe a mother who would take her little one on nature walks? If I expected to be a good parent, what, indeed, would I be good at doing?

The answer came early on in my child's life. Jennifer was but weeks old when I began our nightly ritual of reading *Goodnight Moon*, Margaret Wise Brown's classic, comforting picture book about a bunny settling down for the night. With my baby snug in her jammies, cradled in my lap in the rocking chair with lullabies playing softly at our side, the poetry of *Goodnight Moon* never lost its magic. Ah, I thought, this is what I like about being a mother.

(This was reassuring, because the very idea of planning a birthday party sends my imagination into reverse; I'm easily bored at parks; my three daughters have shown no interest in baseball; carsickness is a family affliction; and nature walks are only an annual event in our household.)

Yes, I'm a *reading* mom. And like many of the extraordinary books my children and I have enjoyed through the years, *Goodnight Moon* did not end with the last page. It lived on in our imaginations as we said good night to all the objects in the nursery and to the people in my baby's universe. I don't know when my daughter realized who her Aunt Janet and Uncle David were. They lived in Massachusetts and we were in California. We saw them but once a year, but we said good night to them every night. A picture book helped make that connection.

Books make us laugh, cry, think. Books have brought our family together. Read-aloud time is sacred in our household, skipped only under the most dire of circumstances (Halloween, for instance). I haven't stopped reading to my children, even though the older two are fully capable of reading to themselves. Jennifer is nearly a teenager; this past summer she and I enjoyed a Philip Pullman mystery about the opium trade in 1870s London, *The Ruby in the Smoke*, after her sisters had been tucked into bed. Jennifer also brought a pillow into her nine-year-old sister Allison's room so she could camp out on the floor while I read aloud *The Exiles*, Hilary McKay's witty and thoughtful novel about four quirky sisters who are shipped off to spend the summer with their equally idiosyncratic grandmother. Jennifer had heard me read this delightful book two years ago, read it to herself a few months later, listened to me read it again, and grabbed it to reread to herself. One novel, four reads, and we're all still giggling about the author's cleverness and debating whether Big Grandma got what was coming to her at the end of the book.

So many of my favorite moments with my children have revolved around reading. I'll never forget the night Allison, then seven, clutched the chapter book we were reading every night and sighed, "Dear *Rusty's Space Ship*. Gosh, I love this book!" I, too, had loved *Rusty's Space Ship* as a child, ever since my third-grade teacher, Mrs. George, had read it to our class every day after lunch. I had searched for years for this charming story of a girl, a boy and a dog touring the solar system before finally tracking down a thirty-five-year-old copy in the library of a nearby town. Just as Mrs. George had done more than thirty years earlier, I read one chapter a day. And Allison was spellbound — captivated by a book that had sparked my interest in space travel and made me certain I would be an astronaut when I grew up. By reading that novel to my daughters I managed to recapture a cherished part of my own childhood, and to create memories for them as well. Some parents may have those experiences at the ballpark; for me they usually take place on the family room couch, courtesy of the public library or my favorite children's bookstore.

When my youngest, Molly, was a year and a half, she was dreadfully ill and wasting away from a chronic illness that took three months to diagnose. That Christmas Molly showed an interest in one gift, her own copy of a book we had checked out of the library several times. It was a miracle that she was paying attention to me reading *Baby Brother Blues*, a tale of sibling rivalry, on Christmas morning, when it was clear her body was conserving energy just to stay alive. Books can do that.

Jennifer and Allison also suffered through that nightmarish period. While not physically ill, they were worried, jealous, angry, guilty, distracted, sad, lonely, and about a dozen other psychologically detrimental things. At times during our ordeal I looked for a book that would address their emotional needs and concerns, but found none. That's what inspired me to write my first published book, *When Molly Was in the Hospital: A Book for Brothers and Sisters of Hospitalized Children*. I couldn't believe there wasn't a picture book for and about siblings of hospitalized children, so I wrote a fictionalized account of our family's experience. The book, which was masterfully illustrated by Nina Ollikainen, MD, has certainly helped each of my children when one of their sisters has been hospitalized (unfortunately, all three have been in the hospital at least once). I'm always gratified when I hear of other families using our book to get through a rough time.

Fortunately, learning to read has come fairly easily to my daughters. When Jennifer wanted more than picture books, I tried to stay at least one step ahead of her. I constantly asked librarians, teachers, and other parents for recommendations of great books. When I volunteered in the school library, I learned who the good readers were and asked them what were their favorite books. As Jennifer picked up her reading speed, she could finish three novels a week before falling asleep at night. During the day I would do my research, so I'd rarely encounter the complaint, "I don't have anything to read!"

I, too, was reading many of these books. I reasoned that if I wanted to write for children, I'd better become familiar with the best. (It's a tough job, I know, but some of us have to do it.) I joined an incredibly talented writers group. I began subscribing to journals and magazines of children's literature, and attending writers conferences and librarians conventions to learn everything I could about what was being published. So many of the books were exciting or thoughtful or hilarious or touching, or just plain worth getting into children's hands. There was some great stuff out there!

After a few years, people began asking *me* for advice on children's books. "My fourth-grade son says he hates to read," a parent would say. "He's only interested in sports."

I tried to be ready with at least two books to recommend. "Have you checked out *The Trading Game?* It's about baseball cards. Or *Yang the Youngest and His Terrible Ear?* The main character in that book wants to play baseball, but his family needs him for their string quartet." Then I'd usually rattle off several of my favorite read-alouds: *The Boggart; Ace: The Very Important Pig; Ginger Pye; Tuck Everlasting*, followed by a few "children's" books that adults would also enjoy: *The Ear, the Eye and the Arm; The Giver;* and *Baby*.

Our school librarian, who by this time had become a friend, asked me to help her develop an annotated list of books (that is, books along with descriptions) to give to all elementary students in the district. Our list was never finished, but the research I conducted helped me even more in developing my own list of recommended books (which did not have to be approved by committee). Finally someone said, "You're so enthusiastic about reading, Debbie. Why don't you try to go on KGO talk radio?"

Ronn Owens hosts the top talk-radio morning show in San Francisco. Once or twice a year he invites people to apply to be "instant guests." All you have to do is call up, pitch a topic to the listening audience, then wait for the on-air vote. Two people out of about twenty win and have to be in the studio by the last hour of the show. I was "Applicant number four" one Memorial Day, described as "Debbie on kids' books," with bags of favorite books packed and ready to go to San Francisco.

I didn't win, but I did come in fourth in the voting (I lost out to a bus driver and an ex-con). I was encouraged enough, though, to write a letter to Ronn proposing a stint as a regular, scheduled guest. The producer called up two months later and offered me a spot.

That's how I came to be known as "the children's book lady." Once or twice a year I've been a guest on Ronn Owens's program, answering questions he has for me and calls from listeners. The show has an audience of about 100,000, so it's an effective way to get the word out on great books for children. I also encourage people to call my publisher for a list of my family's favorite books. Several hundred do so every time I give out the number.

The list I compiled for KGO radio listeners is one I wish I had had five years ago. Going into a bookstore or library can be overwhelming to a parent. Where to start? What's really worth reading? What will turn my child *on* to reading, not turn him off? What books will keep kids wanting to read late into the night, or yearning for the next chapter to be read to them the following day? What books will kids want to talk about? What books will kids clutch and sigh, "Gosh, I love this book!"

My list was a beginning, meant to get kids and parents started in finding books children will enjoy. I was constantly updating and changing it, and because I wanted it to fit on two sides of one sheet of paper, I couldn't ever list *all* of my favorite books. So when my publisher asked me to write a book that would address many of the questions I was asked on the air as well as expand my reading list, I decided to close up the word processing file on the middle-grade novel I had been writing and start a new project. Parents have myriad questions about reading and books. I may not have all the answers, but I can usually get people headed in the right direction.

My goal as a children's literature advocate is to spread contagious enthusiasm for reading as far as it will go. By showing how my family and other families I know have used and enjoyed some of the best contemporary and classic children's books, I hope to give parents a solid foundation for building a family library.

I confess, as a reader and writer I'm quite critical. A lot of what's being published, unfortunately, is not worth buying or reading. A little junk in a reading diet is fine, but there are things parents can do to get their kids to move beyond the popular mega-series offerings. The great books are there — books that will expand a child's horizons and bring magic to her world. Books that have characters with something to say. Books sitting on library and bookstore shelves that deserve to reach a wider audience.

I don't pretend to know the best way to teach the mechanics of reading to all children, and this is not a book about how that is done. The best elementary school teachers, I believe, use a combination of phonics (letter sounds) and whole language (literature-based, including a child's own writing). In California, this so-called balanced approach to reading education became a mandate in 1996. I've observed each of my daughters' first-grade teachers working with students on letter sounds as well as reading aloud to them. At home, I concentrate on the fun stuff — introducing my children to great books by reading with them for at least twenty minutes a day.

Over the past ten years, phonics tapes have been heavily promoted to parents. While this method may work for some children as a supplement to schoolwork and to reading with a parent, I worry that these companies are trying to scare parents into buying a (supposedly) good reading education. There's a danger, too, in that parents who buy into the sales pitch will think their jobs are over once their child has finished the tapes (if, indeed, anyone ever completes the programs). Jennifer used one of the phonics tapes in first grade, after the parents of a student in her class had donated a set because their child refused to pay attention beyond the first lesson. (Like an exercise bike given to Goodwill, the parents wanted their investment to have a little longer life.) My six-year-old listened a few times and began mocking the program. "B — boring, D — dull," Jennifer and two of her friends chanted one day after school.

There is no quick fix to becoming a good reader, and, as this book is all about, reading children's literature is something parents should enjoy with their kids long before and long after their children become fluent readers. I hope parents will highlight, dog-ear and underline this book before taking it to the library and bookstore. (That is, unless it belongs to the library, in which case I recommend my low-tech, proven method of marking pages with strips of scratch paper.) It's never too early — or too late — to introduce children to the joy of reading.

Another wonderful aspect about reading is that both moms and dads (and grandparents and other significant friends and family members) can participate. In our family it turns out that I prefer reading, and my husband, Bill, likes to tell stories. He has a tendency to leave out words, phrases or even — gasp! — entire sentences when reading aloud our kids' favorite books, which I always hear about later. And I have trouble coming up with original bedtime stories — starring the girls, of course, the way Bill does — and resort to reciting a favorite book when called upon to tell a story. It's a division of "labor" that works well for our family. I have one neighbor and friend who reads faithfully to his sons every night. Lucky boys they are, for a study in California found that boys whose fathers read to them are better readers. Now *do* I have your attention?

For a little over a year I wrote a weekly newspaper column about my family for the (now, alas, defunct) *Peninsula Times Tribune* in Palo Alto, California. I wrote about everything: sharing maternity clothes; delivering a baby (Molly's birth was announced to thousands of readers ten days after she was born); hating Halloween; keeping the last name I've had since birth; taking three little ones out to dinner on my own; dealing with bad hair months and sleepless nights; my aging grandmother; explaining cancer or prejudice or war to my children; and, of course, one on the joys of reading. My editor called that column "Just like stepping into a book," and it was about my stumbling into the London neighborhood of our favorite British children's author and illustrator, Shirley Hughes, and half expecting to see one of her characters come walking down the street.

Thinking back, I would have loved to have written every column about reading and books. Now I have that chance. And now I can recommend Peggy Rathmann as well as Shirley Hughes, and Nancy Farmer, Susan Cooper, Chris Crutcher, and so many other authors who write those unforgettable stories for older kids. I can write about bringing the wonderful world of children's books into any family's home. I've turned a passion into a career.

It can be every parent's passion as well. Reading remarkable books with your children is far more rewarding than an exercise-bike approach to the mechanics of reading. It shouldn't be scary or overwhelming. It takes time, but time with kids can't be better spent. Don't give up if your son thinks he hates reading. Read him a good story. Be consistent. It will enrich your family's life in ways you can only imagine. Do it for your children *and* for yourself. ❦

Books

Babbitt, Natalie, *Tuck Everlasting* (1975)

Brown, Margaret Wise, *Goodnight Moon*, illustrated by Clement Hurd (1947)

Cooper, Susan, *The Boggart* (1993)

Duncan, Debbie, *When Molly Was in the Hospital: A Book for Brothers and Sisters of Hospitalized Children*, illustrated by Nina Ollikainen, MD (1994)

Estes, Eleanor, *Ginger Pye* (1951)

Farmer, Nancy, *The Ear, the Eye and the Arm* (1994)

King-Smith, Dick, *Ace: The Very Important Pig*, illustrated by Lynette Hemmant (1990)

Lampman, Evelyn Sibley, *Rusty's Space Ship* (1957)

Lowry, Lois, *The Giver* (1993)

MacLachlan, Patricia, *Baby* (1993)

McKay, Hilary, *The Exiles* (1991)

Namioka, Lensey, *Yang the Youngest and His Terrible Ear*, illustrated by Kees de Kiefte (1992)

Polushkin, Maria, *Baby Brother Blues*, illustrated by Ellen Weiss (1987)

Pullman, Philip, *The Ruby in the Smoke* (1985)

Slote, Alfred, *The Trading Game* (1990)

First Books

After nearly four years of marriage and three miscarriages, Bill and I became parents one foggy January morning in 1985. Soon the gifts began pouring in for Jennifer from family, friends, and colleagues. Among all the sleepers and blankets, we received a set of five Helen Oxenbury board books from our friends Helen and Peter.

Board books? I wondered. Reading from the back covers I learned that baby board books were "... created for babies from the age of six months." Six months??? This was news. I think I had only two books before I started kindergarten: *Nurse Nancy* and *Little Black Sambo* (it was the 1950s). Obviously my friend Helen knew more about children's books for children of baby boomers than I did. Could a baby really care about a book?

You bet she could. We still have *Friends*, *Family*, *Dressing*, *Working*, and *Playing*, the Oxenbury board books that launched our children's book home library. I imagine I turned those sixteen-page books at least two thousand times, showing my daughters the drawings of the round-headed baby and his daily activities. And, judging by the teeth and fingernail marks notched indelibly on the covers, my three babies handled those books quite a bit themselves. That, of course, is the genius of board books — virtually indestructible, visually engaging, and the right size for a young child to hold. I could leave a board book in my daughter's crib during nap time, and not be afraid it would be in pieces (or — worse! — lodged in her throat) an hour later. (Jennifer tore out, page by page, our first copy of Dr. Seuss's *The Cat in the Hat* one day at about age two and a half, when she did *not* want to take her afternoon rest, as only a two-and-a-half-year-old can show that she does *not* want to be left alone to nap.)

My baby was about a month old when I wandered into a children's bookstore for the first time. I felt both comfortable and lost. This was a place I could learn to love, but how would I find my way around? Where should I start? A helpful staff member, undoubtedly sensing my newcomer status (I guess the baby in the front-pack gave me away), handed me a copy of *Goodnight Moon* by Margaret Wise Brown. "Read this," she said. "You'll love it."

"When?" I replied.

"Now, here in the store, and every night to your baby."

"But she's a *baby*. She doesn't understand books yet."

"She will, long before you realize it. Reading aloud is a habit you should start early."

"Even this early?" I asked, pointing to the downy head of my sleeping infant.

She smiled. "Oh, yes," she said. "The owner of our store told us about a wise woman who, when asked how soon parents should start reading to their children, replied, 'I'll let you get off the delivery table. But on the way down the hall . . . .'"

"Whoops. Then I guess I'm already a few weeks late."

"Don't worry," she said. "Just read this book."

I sat down and read *Goodnight Moon*, and was enchanted. Yet, that day I had no idea how many ways and different levels my family would enjoy and appreciate this beloved children's picture book — the poetry, the pictures, saying good night to our own nursery and friends and family, searching for the mouse, even occasionally altering the text. (The old lady hasn't always whispered "Hush" in our household.

Sometimes she shouts, "Wubba wubba!") Through the years we have purchased at least two hardcover copies, several paperback versions, and, when the board book came out, one or two of those as well.

Goodnight Moon showed me that babies and children understand books read aloud to them that are above their "reading level." It's an important lesson that I continue to use to enhance and vary our read-aloud choices. A seven-year-old may be able to read simple children's books on her own, yet she can also appreciate L. M. Montgomery's rather complex Anne of Green Gables when read to her. Conversely, when children are tired or ill, a familiar childhood favorite can provide just the comfort they need. Allison, nine, occasionally asks me to recite all thirty-four lines of Goodnight Moon as I tuck her into bed.

Now there is Peggy Rathmann's Good Night, Gorilla, the silly picture book about seven animals following their zookeeper home for the night. Funny to the bone, Good Night, Gorilla appeals to infants and children (kids get the jokes!), as well as to the all-important adult reader (it's short and soothing, so repeated readings aren't ever boring). Molly was so proud when, at the age of four, she could read the entire book all by herself by using the pictures to help her remember the names of the animals. Peggy Rathmann is a children's book author and illustrator who respects her audience enough to pack a remarkable amount of detail and humor into every page of her picture books. Good Night, Gorilla is also available as a board book — perfect for the crib or car seat.

A few words of caution about board book reprints: Sometimes key elements or pages are left out when a picture book is turned into a board book, so be sure to look carefully and compare both versions, if available, before deciding which to buy. When Molly was two, she used the colored stripes on the endpapers of Bill Martin, Jr. and Eric Carle's Brown Bear, Brown Bear, What Do You See? to give her the clue as to which animal will appear on the next page. She felt like a real reader! What a shame that the stripes didn't make it into the board book version. Bruce Degen's cheerful and playful *Jamberry* is appropriate for the board book crowd, but *It Looked Like Spilt Milk*, Charles Shaw's book for preschoolers about cloud formations, is much too sophisticated a concept for toddlers to appreciate.

Check your library for Rachel Isadora's charming out-of-print collection of books, *I Hear*, *I See*, and *I Touch*. Two are available as "abridged" board books but suffered in the editing process. And if you're like me and appreciate the aesthetics of holding in your hands a silky-smooth, full-sized original of Sam McBratney's *Guess How Much I Love You* while you turn the pages and read to a cuddly child in your lap, splurge a little and go for the hardcover. *Guess How Much I Love You*, the book with the surprisingly soothing back-and-forth nighttime banter between Little Nutbrown Hare and his father about the extent of their mutual affection is, after all, a story whose very premise is based on parent-child interaction. In this mother's opinion, it is a different experience altogether with a clunky, chunky board book.

Babies do care about books, and so should parents. Little ones love to look at board books with pictures of babies and toddlers. They also enjoy the closeness of being held and read to. I've long been convinced that reading aloud to babies helps with language acquisition and future learning. Recent neurological research confirms my beliefs. Babies who are read to are already plugged in, if you will. Every child deserves that advantage. Children's book author and illustrator Rosemary Wells, who spearheaded "the most important twenty minutes of your day!" campaign to promote routine reading aloud to children, considers regular daily reading a public health issue. So does the American Academy of Pediatrics.

Reading is also, without a doubt, a wonderful way to share special time with a child. That alone should be a good enough reason for parents — even busy, busy parents — to make reading to and with children part of their everyday lives. Start early. Ask for books for baby and birthday presents, and give books to others. Borrow books from the library or friends, and look for them at yard sales. You don't have to have a lot of money to promote an early appreciation of books and reading. You just have to care. 🐝

Books

Brown, Margaret Wise, *Goodnight Moon*, illustrated by Clement Hurd (1947)

Degen, Bruce, *Jamberry* (1983)

Isadora, Rachel, *I Hear; I See; I Touch* (1985)

Martin, Bill, Jr., *Brown Bear, Brown Bear, What Do You See?*, illustrated by Eric Carle (1983)

McBratney, Sam, *Guess How Much I Love You*, illustrated by Anita Jeram (1995)

Montgomery, L.M., *Anne of Green Gables* (1908)

Oxenbury, Helen, *Dressing; Family; Friends; Playing; Working* (1981)

Rathmann, Peggy, *Good Night, Gorilla* (1994)

Seuss, Dr., *The Cat in the Hat* (1957)

Shaw, Charles G., *It Looked Like Spilt Milk* (1947)

The Next Step

What a magical, marvelous milestone it is when a young child asks for a particular book, not just any book. Once this happens, no longer will all books automatically go into her mouth, or be tossed out of the shelves and scattered on the floor as if they were any old object. For the child, books are starting to be more than the paper (or cardboard) on which they are printed. He realizes that books have pages with drawings, or perhaps photographs. Books have squiggles that bigger people call "words," words that may rhyme or words that sing. Silly words. Words that sometimes make grown-ups smile, laugh, give a hug, or even cry.

Maybe your daughter will bring you a book you have read together many times. Maybe she will say "More" when you finish reading a favorite one. You'll recognize it when it first happens. Rejoice! Then read the book as many times as she wants, knowing she's on her way to discovering the wonderful world of words, books, and literature.

Dorothy Kunhardt's *Pat the Bunny* is one book that managed to make the successful transition from teething toy to honest-to-goodness book for our girls. And it's interactive! My kids patted that bunny, played peek-a-boo with Paul, smelled the flowers, looked in the mirror, felt Daddy's scratchy face, read (and, unfortunately, also tore) Judy's book, and put their fingers through "Mummy's" ring hundreds of times. (Mummy's??? I always thought. Couldn't the American publisher have changed that? But I tried not to skip a beat.) *Pat the Bunny*, though short on plot, is a book that works.

Nursery rhymes make ideal beginner books. Go to any bookstore and you'll find dozens, from simple board books to comprehensive collections. Jennifer carried around a board book with the plain title of *Nursery Rhymes* (Eloise Wilkin's name appears in a tiny signature on the cover) for months during her second year. This book went everywhere — in the stroller or car seat, to Grandma's, definitely into the crib, and even out to the sandbox. Once, when it was missing for more than an hour (horror of all horrors!), I rushed out to purchase another, backup copy. Jennifer asked Bill or me to read those seven nursery rhymes to her and sing them to her, until — and long after — she could recite and sing them on her own.

While not nearly as portable, *My Very First Mother Goose*, edited by Iona Opie and illustrated by the illustrious Rosemary Wells, is a feast for the eyes and ears. Six-year-old Molly loves to study the drawings of the adorable animals as we read the words together — to rhymes we know and love, or those we're learning to know and love. I keep our copy handy, out on the coffee table.

Sandra Boynton's board books about animals doing and saying the silliest things, especially *The Going To Bed Book* and *Moo, Baa, La La La*, have humor and rhyme to withstand a multitude of readings. *The Going To Bed Book* was Bill's first favorite children's book to read to our daughters; when called upon, he can still recite the entire text. All one of us has to say is, "The moon has set not long ago, now everybody goes below . . . " and Bill takes it from there. His animated readings, while not necessarily lulling the girls to sleep, let them know that their dad enjoys books. All moms and dads should look for such books, particularly if they are not the primary read-aloud parent. Read the ones that *you* especially like, and your child will pick up on your enthusiasm.

The cheerful illustrations in Shirley Hughes's "Nursery Collection" are equally matched by its delightful rhymes. These are the books I reached for when my kids were little. Fortunately, I bought *Colors, Noisy, Bathwater's Hot,* and *Two Shoes, New Shoes* when they were still in print; I recommend searching for these charming books at the library. Children and parents who come to love those Shirley Hughes characters can look forward to graduating to meet Alfie and Annie Rose, the sibling stars of *Alfie Gives a Hand, Alfie Gets in First, Alfie's Feet, An Evening at Alfie's, The Big Alfie and Annie Rose Storybook, The Big Alfie Out of Doors Storybook,* and *Rhymes for Annie Rose.* Our well-thumbed copy of *Alfie Gives a Hand,* the tale of Alfie the preschooler insisting on taking his blanket to a birthday party, still has Allison's name and phone number in it. She was our blanket-toting child, and I recall vividly her need to have the book with her at preschool when her baby sister Molly was ill. Every time I read *Alfie Gets in First,* my girls insist I tell the story of two-year-old Jennifer locking me out of *our* house.

Rosemary Wells thoughtfully wrote three books in the *Voyage to the Bunny Planet* collection, and Jennifer, Allison, and Molly have already decided which volumes they will inherit. My kids absolutely adore these books, which we have in a small, boxed set. Each book begins with a poor, tormented bunny having a horrendous day. When transported to the Bunny Planet, however, Robert, Claire and Felix find warmth, serenity and love — in rhyme, no less. When Molly was just two and had to be hospitalized for the fourth time in less than a year, she kept the Bunny Planet books on her bed. Young as she was, Molly somehow knew that better times would come her way. *Voyage to the Bunny Planet* seemed to reassure her that even really sick or disastrous days don't last forever, that she had something to look forward to. That's not a bad concept for the very young — or anyone, for that matter — to master.

Toddlers love familiarity, and we welcomed the characters from *Sesame Street* into our home in book as well as television form. Among our favorites: *I Want to Go Home*, in which Big Bird gets a bad case of homesickness while visiting Granny Bird; *Bert and the Missing Mop Mix-Up*, where the *Sesame Street* gang unwittingly plays the classic children's game of "telephone" while Bert waits for something to clean up the spilled milk; and *Nobody Cares About Me*, the story of Big Bird's jealousy of the attention heaped upon his sick friend Ernie.

Eric Hill's lift-the-flap books starring Spot the puppy, beginning with *Where's Spot?*, were also popular with our girls when they were toddlers. For rhythm, rhyme, and fun, we often pulled out *Wheel Away!* by Dayle Ann Dodds, illustrated by Thacher Hurd. It's the tale of a bicycle wheel "pa-da-rump, pa-da-rump, pa-da-rump-pump-pump'ing through town. Bill Martin, Jr. and Eric Carle's *Brown Bear, Brown Bear, What Do You See?* is a brilliant book of repetitions, simple enough for a two-year-old to memorize — especially with the help of the colored stripes on the inside of the back and front covers.

Goodnight Moon was the first of many popular modern bedtime books for children. There must be as many going-to-bed stories as there are nursery rhyme books. It has something to do, of course, with the major goal of almost every parent of a young child at the end of a day: sleep . . . for everyone. A regular routine of bedtime reading, ending with a soothing story, is comforting for child and parent alike.

Check out several bedtime books to find those that appeal to you. After *Goodnight Moon* we added *Good Night, Gorilla* to our repertoire. On many nights we still snuggle up with *Guess How Much I Love You*. And Molly is especially fond of *Night Sounds* by Lois Grambling, illustrated by Randall Ray. Its gentle, reassuring tone would calm even the most anxious one- or two-year-old.

Whether it is poetry or story, interactivity or lullabyability, books for the very young can become lifelong friends and companions. Seek out the best and never stop looking. Your child's first favorite books are just around the corner. ❦

Books

Boynton, Sandra, *Moo, Baa, La La La* (1982); *The Going to Bed Book* (1982)

Brown, Margaret Wise, *Goodnight Moon*, illustrated by Clement Hurd (1947)

Dodds, Dayle Ann, *Wheel Away!*, illustrated by Thacher Hurd (1989)

Grambling, Lois G., *Night Sounds*, illustrated by Randall F. Ray (1996)

Hill, Eric, *Where's Spot?* (1980); *Spot Goes to School* (1984); *Spot Goes to the Beach* (1989)

Hughes, Shirley, *Noisy* (1985); *Bathwater's Hot* (1985); *Colors* (1986); *Alfie Gets in First* (1981); *Alfie's Feet* (1982); *Alfie Gives a Hand* (1983); *An Evening at Alfie's* (1984); *The Big Alfie and Annie Rose Storybook* (1988); *The Big Alfie Out of Doors Storybook* (1992); *Rhymes for Annie Rose* (1995)

Kunhardt, Dorothy, *Pat the Bunny* (1940)

Martin, Bill, Jr., *Brown Bear, Brown Bear, What Do You See?*, illustrated by Eric Carle (1983)

McBratney, Sam, *Guess How Much I Love You*, illustrated by Anita Jeram (1995)

Opie, Iona, *My Very First Mother Goose*, illustrated by Rosemary Wells (1996)

Rathmann, Peggy, *Good Night, Gorilla* (1994)

Roberts, Sarah, *Nobody Cares About Me* (1982); *Bert and the Missing Mop Mix-Up* (1983); *I Want to Go Home* (1985), all illustrated by Joe Mathieu

Wells, Rosemary, *Voyage to the Bunny Planet: First Tomato, Moss Pillows, The Island Light* (1992)

Wilkin, Eloise, *Nursery Rhymes* (1979)

Picture Books for Kids Just Starting to Sit Still

For my first five years as a mom, I worked in an office every morning while Jennifer and Allison stayed home with a baby sitter or went to nursery school near our house. It worked out well for me, until finding new part-time child care managed to become a full-time job in itself. One night I tendered my resignation — by e-mail, no less.

I cherished my afternoons during those early years. Having had my daily fix of the adult world, I returned home happy to be Mom again. Clara, Shelly or Christina, three of our loving and talented sitters (we had another horrific child care provider, who shall remain nameless, for three seemingly long months) had already taken the girls to the park, played games with them, and sat them down for lunch. The children were fed, happy, and ready for play and reading with Mom before their afternoon rest. All things considered, not a bad life.

When Jennifer became bored with lifting the flaps in her books, I decided to try moving on to the next level — stories that might actually have plot, character, and conflict. My toddler, naturally, didn't think of *Madeline* as literature. She simply enjoyed the silly rhyming story in the big, colorful book about the little girl in Paris with red hair who had to have her appendix out. Her friends were jealous and naturally wanted to have their appendixes out too. This book has real kid-like emotions that ring true more than fifty years after its publication. My children may live thousands of miles away from Paris and Madeline's boarding-school culture, but they still love Madeline, the spunky kid who just says "Pooh-pooh" to the tiger in the zoo. Madeline was my girls' first literary role model. Her story is universal in the best definition of the word.

We read all the Madeline books, but the original and *Madeline's Christmas* remain our favorites. Jennifer had memorized the entire text of *Madeline* at the age of two, and by seven she had come up with a rap version after listening to me read it again to Molly. I look at Ludwig Bemelmans's illustrations and think that I should be able to draw children the way he does, but of course I can't. Simple is not the same as simplistic.

Don Freeman's *Corduroy* is another character we fell in love with on those sleepy afternoons. Corduroy, the department store bear who wants a home, a button, and a friend, finds all of those and more with the help of Lisa, the girl who loves him, regardless of his faults. Corduroy gets lost again in the sequel, *A Pocket for Corduroy*, which is just as charming as the original story. No matter that big-city department stores and laundromats with Bohemian artists are not part of my children's everyday life. Of course they identify with Lisa, because she wants a small bear in green overalls enough to spend all she's saved in her piggy bank. Looking new isn't important to a child. Lisa is devastated at the thought of losing Corduroy at the laundromat, just as two-year-old Allison cried for the entire afternoon when her own bear, Albert, was missing in a pile of newspapers. Stuffed animals can be real friends to children. And Corduroy only wants what everyone else has — a home, some love, and a pocket. Every kid knows that pants or overalls aren't any good without pockets. Without pockets, where would you keep all the junk?

Jan Ormerod's *Sunshine* is a wordless picture book with a lot to say about family life and routines. Even toddlers can figure out the story of the young girl as she casually leads her parents through the first hour or so of their morning. The first to wake up, she is the one who warns Dad of the burning toast and proves sufficiently grown up to get herself dressed and ready for school while her parents are still enjoying breakfast in bed. Finally, she reminds her mother and father of the time — which, of course, causes the old folks to run around like mad to get their own selves ready to leave the house. This book is full of warmth, humor, and love. We made up our own words and came up with open-ended questions every time we read *Sunshine*. ("Uh-oh, do you think Daddy will stop reading the paper and see the burning toast? . . . Whoops, will Mom and Dad be late for work? . . . What do you think is happening here?") I knew that when my girls took this book to bed, they were telling themselves their own stories. A friend of mine, a mother who is a professor of psychology, declared, "*Sunshine* is a masterpiece." The sequel, *Moonlight*, is about the same family settling down for the night in a decidedly nonlinear fashion. (This seems the appropriate place to confess that Bill and I have each fallen asleep while reading to or telling our daughters a story before bed.)

The first "science" book my children enjoyed was Eric Carle's *The Very Hungry Caterpillar*, a story of a captivating caterpillar who eats his way through holes in the pages of the book. Okay, I know caterpillars don't eat " . . . one piece of chocolate cake, one ice-cream cone, one pickle . . . " (do they?), but any kid who does surely will wind up with the same kind of stomachache. This is an ingenious book that appeals to one-year-olds who like to turn the partial pages of the fruit the caterpillar has eaten through on Monday through Friday (hey! toddlers are also learning the days of the week), and put their fingers through the holes as the caterpillar continues his Saturday eating frenzy. Children who are ready to start kindergarten pride themselves in knowing that caterpillars build cocoons and emerge as big, beautiful butterflies about two weeks later. Where did kids first learn about the life cycle of a butterfly? Most likely from *The Very Hungry Caterpillar*.

Perhaps the most famous peddler in early childhood literature is to be found in Esphyr Slobodkina's cherished and classic tale, *Caps for Sale*. As the story goes, a peddler loses his stack of caps to a bunch of monkeys while he stops to nap by a tree. My kids enjoyed this book, I think, because they felt they had the solution to the peddler's problem all figured out, and just wanted to tell him, "Look, you silly grownup, all you have to do is throw your own cap down on the ground, and the monkeys will copy you and give you back all the other caps." Monkey see, monkey do. *Caps for Sale* gives children, well, empowerment. That and predictability: the caps must be arranged in the same color order — with the red caps on the very top — just as Allison's stuffed animals have to sit in a certain order on her shelf.

Robert McCloskey's *Blueberries for Sal* is a warm-hearted, blue-and-white picture book about Little Sal and Little Sal's mother, and Little Bear and Little Bear's mother, who end up all mixed up on Blueberry Hill one day. Little Sal is an irresistible child, just a tad naughty for eating instead of saving the blueberries she picks and for wandering away from her mother. And who beats a hasty retreat when the humans and bears come face to face? Why, the mothers! Little Sal and Little Bear are the real winners in this affectionate tale and portrayal of mid-twentieth-century life.

Blueberries for Sal and another McCloskey winner, *One Morning in Maine*, the book about Sal spending the morning with her father and losing her first tooth, made such an impact on Jennifer that she longed from about the age of two to visit Maine. (Or go to college there, or, perhaps, live the rest of her life there.) Maine isn't exactly within easy driving distance of the West Coast, so it wasn't until the summer before Jennifer began sixth grade that my brother David and his wife, Janet, were able to take her back to Boston, and to

Janet's family's cabin on Loud's Island off the coast of Maine. For a week Jennifer explored the island with her aunt and Janet's other nieces. She stuck her toe in the ice-cold Atlantic, rode on a tractor driven by a nine-year-old cousin, traipsed through the island cemetery where Grandma Maxfield is buried, took a motorboat to the penny candy store on shore, and . . . learned the Macarena. She also picked berries. Of *course* she picked berries. No bears, but still, a dream realized.

It was a dream that began with a book read over and over on lazy afternoons when Jennifer was two years old. I had no idea at the time how much she would remember. But she did. ❦

Books

Bemelmans, Ludwig, *Madeline* (1938); *Madeline's Christmas* (1956)
Carle, Eric, *The Very Hungry Caterpillar* (1969)
Freeman, Don, *Corduroy* (1968); *A Pocket for Corduroy* (1978)
McCloskey, Robert, *Blueberries for Sal* (1948); *One Morning in Maine* (1952)
Ormerod, Jan, *Sunshine* (1981); *Moonlight* (1982)
Slobodkina, Esphyr, *Caps for Sale* (1940)

Picture Books for the Preschool Crowd

From what I have observed, there are two ages when kids who love books can't seem to get enough of them. First, when they're about three and have a desire to work their way through nearly every picture book in the library, and then again, between about seven and ten when their reading skills pick up rapidly, and they'll spend hours at a time with their noses "stuck in a book." At both stages children often discover favorite authors or series, and need constant replenishment of their supply of reading material. Parents can help by making sure enough books are available. Even with the enormous quantity of children's books being published every year (currently around five thousand), there are standouts on the shelves that children choose as their favorite books and want to read — or hear — again and again.

Preschoolers usually aren't picky about the types of books they love. They like stories about animals, about kids *and* animals, about kids, about kids who want animals, and about kids disguised as animals. They like stories about faraway places. They also like clever alphabet and counting books, and books about things they are especially fond of (and sometimes obsessed with), be they dinosaurs, monsters, princesses; trucks, trains, or airplanes. Children enjoy exploring cause and effect, following a concept through to its logical — or illogical — conclusion.

In *If You Give a Mouse a Cookie*, a lucky little boy finds out what might happen if you do just that. Mind you, this mouse is not any old mouse, he practically jumps off the page with appeal and zest as he entices the boy to go along with every "if" (you do this), "when" (you then do that), "then" (something happens), and "so" (guess what? you're back to the beginning!). The whimsical story is as clever as the illustrations, drawing young readers in by addressing them as "you," giving them the feeling that this could happen to any child who gives a cookie to an overall-clad mouse. Laura Joffe Numeroff and Felicia Bond's follow-up tale, *If You Give a Moose a Muffin*, maintains the same charm.

Remy Charlip's time-tested and kid-tested *Fortunately* follows a boy's "good news" and "bad news" experiences on the way to a surprise party. Just when young children think the boy is going to be okay on a "Fortunately . . . " colorful, two-page spread, it's followed by two pages illustrated in black and white that begin with (Uh-oh!) "Unfortunately . . . " Fortunately prevails (fortunately), as the boy happily arrives at his own birthday party. Children take a deep breath at the end of this book, then inevitably ask to hear it again.

Another boy who has a series of unfortunate events in one day is, of course, Alexander, of *Alexander and the Terrible, Horrible, No Good, Very Bad Day*. Judith Viorst lets kids in on a secret known to every adult, namely that " . . . some days are like that." Then she has Alexander add: "Even in Australia." (Which is where Alexander would probably rather be.) This is a book we often read at the end of a rotten day. If the story doesn't cheer my girls up, the illustrations certainly bring a smile or two. I always point out how incredibly late '60s/early '70s the drawings are. My mother took me to school in a VW Beetle just like the car pool driver's (ours was green), and many of my high school friends had "ecology" posters in their bedrooms. I'm delighted to see cultural history preserved for future generations in a timeless story such as Alexander's.

Siblings strike again in Bernard Waber's *Ira Sleeps Over*. Ira's sister insists that Reggie will laugh if Ira takes his teddy bear to his first sleepover at Reggie's house next door. Ira can't figure out whether or not to take his bear, until he finally decides, frown-faced, to leave Tah Tah at home. The prospect of being teased prevails. Then, when the lights are out and the ghost story is over, Reggie gets up to get his own teddy bear, with the apt name of Foo Foo. Suddenly wiser and certainly more secure, Ira marches back home to announce to his mother, his father, and his no-longer know-it-all sister that he has changed his mind. Hooray for Ira! We knew all along he should take his teddy bear, but he needs to make that decision for himself. All kids do.

The back-and-forth banter in *Ira Sleeps Over* reminds me of the Abbott and Costello comedy routine, "Who's on First?" The same style, humor, tension, and heckler are all there in *Ira Says Goodbye*, when Ira and Reggie prepare for Reggie to move away to the world's supposedly greatest town, Greendale. Jennifer loved *Ira Says Goodbye* when she was three, and then went back to it five years later after her own forever-best-friend, Leah, moved to State College, Pennsylvania. Leah had been to all of Jennifer's birthday parties (even the first, when they sat on the floor because neither could walk yet), and they had had the same teacher three years out of four. So when we started hearing about how "great, great, great" State College was, we remembered how sad Ira had felt. And while talking on the telephone isn't the same as seeing someone every day, it does help. So do occasional visits. "State College *is* pretty cool, Mom," Jennifer, age eleven, decided after her first transcontinental trip. Ira couldn't have said it better.

Leah's new home has something Jennifer and her sisters have never seen at their house: snow. It hasn't snowed in our town in more than twenty years, and I find it particularly annoying when books, magazines, and class projects — even in temperate California! — equate winter with snow. A California preschooler may actually never put on a snowsuit, and still live a perfectly normal life. She probably will not, however, be able to avoid cutting out snowflakes in school, or drawing a snowman when asked to illustrate winter.

Given the pet-peeve status snow has for me, I have to admit that Ezra Jack Keats's *The Snowy Day* has won my heart about five hundred times over, and my children's as well. There isn't a better book to illustrate the wonders of a snowy day to a young child, especially to one who has no idea what it is like to crunch or drag a stick through the snow, or to try (in vain) to save a snowball for the next day. My daughters also enjoyed following Peter in the other books about his everyday life, *Whistle for Willie* and *Peter's Chair*.

Maurice Sendak broke the mold in children's books in 1963 with *Where the Wild Things Are*, now a classic preschool favorite. Max is wild, he is angry, and he has power. His imagination makes it possible for him to tame the Wild Things he conjures up in his head *and* to deal with his mother's concrete punishment of sending him to bed without any supper. *Where the Wild Things Are* says to kids that it's okay to be angry. You may get a time out, but you can use that time to go places in your mind where you are king (or queen). Best of all, your mother will forgive you. Supper will be waiting, and it will still be hot.

Dogs and stuffed animals figure prominently in books for preschoolers. Shirley Hughes's *Dogger*, one of our all-time favorites, is a book about a stuffed dog — Dave's dog, Dave's absolutely favorite thing in the whole wide world. So after Dogger becomes "quite lost," Dave is miserable. (That's something we can identify with.) When Dave finally finds Dogger for sale (!) at the school fair, he is frantic, for the lady at the table won't listen to him, and he doesn't have enough money to buy back his toy. To add to the suspense, by the time Dave locates his big sister, Bella, and they return to the table, Dogger has just been bought by a little girl. All ends well, though, thanks to Bella's quick thinking and generosity. Whew! Thank goodness all siblings aren't as mischievous as Ira's. Bella gives big sisters a far better name.

How many young children do *not* want a dog? May, the girl in Dayal Kaur Khalsa's *I Want a Dog*, thinks of nothing else and wants her dog *right now*, not when she's older. She devises an ingenious inanimate solution — a roller skate on a "leash" — that works quite well until her parents no longer say "No" to her requests.

Alex is the little boy in Debra Keller's *The Trouble With Mister* who wants a dog more than anything but is told by his family that a dog is too much trouble. Alex's solution? To paint a picture of the dog of his dreams and name him Mister. The problem is, one night the folded-up Mister turns into a real-life Mister and *really* gets into trouble. Then he runs away! Naturally Alex wants Mister back, even the old, dog-eared Mister that lived mostly in Alex's imagination. *The Trouble With Mister* is a story chock-full of gentle humor and fantasy, ending with a joyful reunion of boy and dog.

There must be hundreds of alphabet books in print. My kids' hands-down top choice when they were young was Bill Martin, Jr. and John Archambault's *Chicka Chicka Boom Boom*. It's an alphabet book, a rhyming book, and an extremely witty and colorful book that reads out loud like a song as the letters (or are they really characters?) of the alphabet all try to climb to the top of the coconut tree. To quote the letter D, "Whee!"

Older children can learn from and appreciate alphabet books as well. One that is remarkably instructive is Cynthia Chin-Lee's *A is for Asia*, illustrated by Yumi Heo. *A is for Asia* is a gracefully written, beautifully illustrated tour of a vast and diverse continent, using letters of the alphabet to describe animals, arts, beliefs, foods, games, living conditions, traditions, and even the weather of Asia. My favorite page is D, for dragon boats; Allison likes A, for Asia; Jennifer and Molly, though, stray from their initials and go for P, for panda.

Another stunning alphabet book is David Pelletier's *The Graphic Alphabet*. In this gorgeous offering, the letter becomes the image it represents, beginning with A crumbling in an avalanche, through K tied in a knot and a trio of O's suspended as ornaments, all the way to a zigzag of a Z. Obviously, alphabet books are not just for kids!

There are some children who freely speak their mind, no matter what the consequences. That's my Allison. When she was six, a commuter train we were taking into San Francisco for a Christmas shopping expedition suddenly stopped in a long tunnel. Word came down ominously through the crowded cars in the pitch-black darkness that "the police are looking for a suspect." No one said anything until Allison cried out: "I want to go home!"

Thinking fast (and wondering along with my friend Catherine, Leah's mom, if we and our five children should duck and cover), I whispered to the kids, "Allison sounds like Bill in *Owl Babies*, doesn't she? Remember, all he said until his mother returned was, 'I want my mommy!'"

"Are we gonna be okay?" mumbled three-year-old Molly.

"Sarah and Percy and Bill were, weren't they?" I replied, biding my time and reminding them of the story of the baby owl siblings who stuck together throughout the night, trying not to think about their mother's absence. By the end of the tale, the lights came on and the train began to move. We all felt like jumping up and down, not on a branch, as the owl babies did upon seeing their mother, but in the aisles of the train.

Owl Babies reassures little ones that Mom will return — from work, from shopping, from a night out with Dad. It also got us through a whopper of a scary situation.

Books can do that, all the time. 🍎

Books

Charlip, Remy, *Fortunately* (1964)
Chin-Lee, Cynthia, *A is for Asia*, illustrated by Yumi Heo (1997)
Hughes, Shirley, *Dogger* (1988)
Keats, Ezra Jack, *Peter's Chair* (1967); *The Snowy Day* (1962); *Whistle for Willie* (1964)

Keller, Debra, *The Trouble with Mister*, illustrated by Shannon McNeill (1995)

Khalsa, Dayal Kaur, *I Want a Dog* (1987)

Martin, Bill, Jr. and John Archambault, *Chicka Chicka Boom Boom*, illustrated by Lois Ehlert (1989)

Numeroff, Laura Joffe, *If You Give a Mouse a Cookie* (1985); *If You Give a Moose a Muffin* (1991), both illustrated by Felicia Bond

Pelletier, David, *The Graphic Alphabet* (1996)

Sendak, Maurice, *Where the Wild Things Are* (1963)

Viorst, Judith, *Alexander and the Terrible, Horrible, No Good, Very Bad Day*, illustrated by Ray Cruz (1972)

Waber, Bernard, *Ira Sleeps Over* (1972); *Ira Says Goodbye* (1988)

Waddell, Martin, *Owl Babies*, illustrated by Patrick Benson (1992)

Picture Books for All Ages

When talking about the audience for picture books, we tend to think of fairly young children who need illustrations to accompany a story. Period. Even though publishers often put an age range of, say, four to eight on a picture book, elementary school children — or perhaps even adults — wouldn't be caught dead enjoying a "picture book," would they?

You bet they would, especially if the author happens to be Chris Van Allsburg, William Steig, or Peggy Rathmann; Kevin Henkes, Patricia Polacco, or the incomparable team of Jon Scieszka and Lane Smith. How about Dr. Seuss? I always thought *The Cat in the Hat* was a little too lengthy (not to mention stimulating) for bedtime reading when my kids were little. As the girls got older and had longer attention spans, they appreciated the humor and stuck with the story, and we all had a heck of a time.

Allison's friend Courtney proudly used a picture book for her first book report in fourth grade. Her copy of Chris Van Allsburg's *The Polar Express* was worn and obviously loved. "It's a book about believing," she told me after school, with a silver bell jingling in her pocket. "The pictures are big and beautiful, and they make me feel like I'm right there on the train going to the North Pole." This modern classic is a perennial best seller and favorite of all ages because the story and art are so enchanting, so magical, so unforgettable. Van Allsburg's *Jumanji* became a household word when Robin Williams turned it into a movie, yet the book about a couple of bored children who discover a board game that transforms their house into a veritable jungle is exciting enough to stand on its own.

People who edit, study, or write children's books often compile lists of their own favorite children's books; when they do, inevitably the lists include a William Steig title. A prominent New York editor told some five hundred children's writers at a conference that *The Amazing Bone* was on his best books list. It is the tale of a talking, music-making magic bone that enriches and ultimately saves the life of sweet young Pearl the pig. I've long been partial to *Sylvester and the Magic Pebble* (and not only because Sylvester's family name is Duncan). In this Steig book, a lovable, pebble-collecting donkey finds one that grants wishes. It's a glorious thing, until Sylvester is frightened by a "mean, hungry lion," panics, and wishes to be a rock. Alas, a rock he remains while his worried parents search in vain for him. The seasons pass until Mr. and Mrs. Duncan find the magic pebble, place it on Sylvester the rock, and wish for the best. Hooray! Sylvester is a donkey again, and all is right with the world.

My kids, though, go along with my brother Brent, father of Lindsey and professor of school psychology, who chooses *Doctor De Soto* as his favorite Steig title. *Doctor De Soto* is the story of a mouse dentist and his wife/assistant who outfox a fox in need of an extraction. When I read that book out loud I sometimes laugh uncontrollably during the first few pages, which makes Molly say, "Mom! Stop laughing so I can hear the words."

William Steig was sixty years old and a long-time cartoonist for *The New Yorker* when he wrote his first children's book. This explains, I think, why some of his sentences — or sentence fragments, even — read like a laugh-out-loud *New Yorker* cartoon. The choice of words! And the stories! Sylvester the donkey's predicament is real as well as magical and, well, funny. It's impossible not to care deeply about him and his parents, as we also root for Pearl and her new-found magic bone. Doctor and Mrs. De Soto remain true to their mouse characters even as they devise a way both to cure the dandy fox's toothache and keep said patient from enjoying them for dinner. Remarkable.

We didn't discover Peggy Rathmann until *Good Night, Gorilla*, so going back to find *Ruby the Copycat* was like unearthing buried treasure. Ruby is the new kid in Miss Hart's class who copies everything about Angela, the girl who sits in front of her. Angela is flattered — temporarily. Ruby switches and copies her teacher, until Miss Hart helps Ruby realize that she, Ruby, has talents of her own. I believe there's a little of Ruby the copycat in each of us. In my case, I recall clearly at age ten becoming so enamored with the Swedish actress Inger Stevens on the new TV show, *The Farmer's Daughter*, that I walked around for about a week saying "Ja" for "Yes." My brothers figured out the "coincidence," and harassed me mercilessly. Of course I denied everything. Copycats usually do.

It was no surprise to our family when Peggy Rathmann won the Caldecott Medal in 1996 for *Officer Buckle and Gloria*. (The Caldecott Medal is awarded annually to the artist of the most distinguished American picture book published during the preceding year.) We were already smitten with Officer Buckle, the likable yet boring Napville police officer who puts students to sleep with his earnest safety speeches, and his new canine sidekick, Gloria, who spices up the talks considerably by acting out the tips behind Officer Buckle's back. Suddenly the students are sitting up and paying attention! "Officer Buckle loved having a buddy" until . . . he sees himself — and Gloria's act — on the nightly news. Whoops! Gloria tries to go it alone, but Gloria without Officer Buckle is the same as Officer Buckle without Gloria: dullsville. With humor and warmth, this book shows children that in many cases the whole may be stronger than each part on its own. "Always stick with your buddy" is a safety tip as well as advice for happy and successful living. Not bad, I'd say, for a thirty-two-page picture book.

Kevin Henkes's mice characters are as lovable as they are believable. Lilly, who stars in *Julius, the Baby of the World* and *Lilly's Purple Plastic Purse*, is charmingly self-centered. It's difficult to find a better children's book than *Julius* about the jealousy an older sibling feels about a new baby. Lilly is as unaccepting of her baby brother as a big sister can be. Then, their cousin actually *agrees* with her negative assessment of baby Julius. Suddenly Julius is "the baby of the world," and Lilly commands Cousin Garland to repeat the proclamation after her. Lilly's feelings are always close to the surface, whether she disdains her "stinky baby brother" or adores her "sharp" new teacher, Mr. Slinger, in *Lilly's Purple Plastic Purse*. She adores him, that is, until he has the nerve to take away her new prized possessions so she won't disturb the class.

Chrysanthemum, Henkes's mouse-girl with the thirteen-letter floral name, must put up with the taunts and chants of the other girls in her class, until a marvelous music teacher by the name of Delphinium Twinkle makes everyone (including Chrysanthemum) look at Chrysanthemum in a more favorable light. *Chrysanthemum* speaks to anyone who has ever been on the giving or receiving end of teasing. (I know some middle school students who could use it as a reminder.)

The prolific Patricia Polacco produces books that are constantly going in and out of the school library where I volunteer. *Chicken Sunday*, the autobiographical tale of young Patricia's endearing friendship with an African-American family in her hometown of Oakland, is our family's favorite. I cannot read Polacco's poignant Civil War story, a tribute to the memory of Pinkus Aylee, *Pink and Say*, without crying. *The Keeping Quilt*, another treasure, is about preserving a family's heritage by passing a quilt from mother to daughter through the generations. Thank goodness Patricia Polacco doesn't keep her family's quilt and their stories only to herself; by sharing her history in picture book form, she enriches readers' lives the world over.

Another memorable picture book involving a quilt (and there are many in children's literature) is Faith Ringgold's *Tar Beach*, the story of a girl who dreams of flying over her hometown of Harlem. Molly likes it because the narrator appears to fly. I marvel at the quilt borders and the uplifting story about the power of imagination.

The glorious paintings in Allen Say's Caldecott Award winner, *Grandfather's Journey*, are complemented perfectly by the moving, almost poetic narrative. Adults usually recognize the feeling of longing for an old home and friends that Say so brilliantly evokes in this picture book, and children learn, as they also do by reading Polacco, about the incredible bond that can exist between the generations.

Many of the finest children's picture books celebrate the ordinary in extraordinary ways. *The Paperboy* by Dav Pilkey is an excellent example. I love the colorful paintings on the pages of this book about a boy and his dog who rise from a warm bed to deliver Saturday morning papers to a dark, sleepy town, and return home to crawl back into bed and dream. I always wanted to be a paperboy like my brother Brent's friend Billy. He was the first kid in the neighborhood to own a ten-speed bike, and he bought it with his own money. I imagine Billy dreamed of that bike when he went back to sleep after delivering his morning papers. I hope he and his children know about *The Paperboy*.

I was first introduced to Janell Cannon's *Stellaluna* by the owner of my local children's bookstore. "Look at this, Debbie," she said, handing it to me. "It's my favorite book of the season." I bought it, and that night I gathered my three kids on the couch to read the story of the baby fruit bat who is raised as a bird after being attacked by an owl. By the time we reached the end of the book, we had gone from being sad (the crisis happens near the beginning) to hopeful, to laughing out loud as Stellaluna tries to be like a bird ("How embarrassing!" she thinks when she can't land gracefully on a branch). What's wrong for a bird may be right for a bat, Stellaluna learns when she is reunited with her mother and other bats. Still, she can be friends with the birds, even though they look at the world from an entirely different angle (who is upside down, really?).

"That's a *great* book," Jennifer declared. About half a million California elementary students agreed with her a few years later, as *Stellaluna* won the 1996 California Young Reader Medal.

When former schoolteacher Jon Scieszka teamed up with artist and illustrator Lane Smith in *The True Story of the Three Little Pigs*, adjectives attempting to describe their work began to fill the book reviews: zany, innovative, sophisticated, hilarious, outrageous, dark, satirical, and clever among them. Suddenly a new style of children's picture book was on the shelves. Scieszka and Smith's next offerings, *The Stinky Cheese Man & Other Fairly Stupid Tales* and *Math Curse*, are also delightfully irreverent and incredibly appealing to older children and adults who appreciate parody and modern abstract art.

A friend of mine buys *The True Story of the Three Little Pigs* for lawyers (the wolf was framed, or so he contends). *The Stinky Cheese Man* turns book design on its side and retells fairy tales in such an entertaining way that fourth-grade boys line up to request it. *Math Curse* is worth studying and enjoying, especially for those of us who occasionally suffer from math anxiety. The narrator's dilemma of seeing everything as a math problem reminds me of the day in high school when I realized I could finally touch-type; every time I had a thought, I typed out the words in my mind. I nearly went crazy! Certainly, I could have used Scieszka and Smith to write me out of my conundrum. ("Smith" is immensely easier to type than "Scieszka," by the way.) What will this pair come up with next? I can't wait to find out.

Many of the best picture books are, indeed, for all ages. ❦

Books

Cannon, Janell, *Stellaluna* (1993)

Henkes, Kevin, *Julius, the Baby of the World* (1990); *Chrysanthemum* (1991); *Lilly's Purple Plastic Purse* (1996)

Pilkey, Dav, *The Paperboy* (1996)

Polacco, Patricia, *The Keeping Quilt* (1988); *Chicken Sunday* (1992); *Pink and Say* (1994)

Rathmann, Peggy, *Ruby the Copycat* (1991); *Good Night, Gorilla* (1994); *Officer Buckle and Gloria* (1995)

Ringgold, Faith, *Tar Beach* (1991)

Say, Allen, *Grandfather's Journey* (1993)

Scieszka, Jon, *The True Story of the 3 Little Pigs* (1989); *The Stinky Cheese Man & Other Fairly Stupid Tales* (1992); *Math Curse* (1995), all illustrated by Lane Smith

Seuss, Dr., *The Cat in the Hat* (1957)

Steig, William, *Sylvester and the Magic Pebble* (1969); *The Amazing Bone* (1976); *Doctor De Soto* (1982)

Van Allsburg, Chris, *Jumanji* (1981); *The Polar Express* (1985)

Read-aloud Favorites

Parents who regularly read to their children inevitably decide one day that their son or daughter is ready for more than "just" picture books. Perhaps the child can sit still longer, perhaps he's been asking for books with longer stories, or perhaps it's the parent who wants books with lengthier or more complex plots. I don't think anyone ever really outgrows the best picture books, but books with more than thirty-two, forty, or sixty-four pages have so much to offer that I consider it a real milestone when my child can maintain interest in a book through twenty or so chapters.

Which books to choose can, however, be tricky. Trickier than with picture books, because if the story doesn't work, a lot more time and emotional energy have been invested in it. Although, I must add, that I'll stop reading a book if we all give it thumbs down, and I advise my friends to do the same, even if it's a book I've recommended to them. Stop. Quit. Try another. Don't waste your time or your child's time reading something you don't enjoy. There are too many other choices available.

Jennifer and I will never forget the failure of our first major read-aloud. What was it? E. B. White's *Charlotte's Web*, one of the best books ever published for children, a book so astonishingly well crafted that I felt as if I, a children's book writer in training, should be taking notes. Four-year-old Jennifer and I sat transfixed night after night on an uncomfortable mini-futon in the room she shared with two-year-old Allison, falling in love with Charlotte and Wilbur. "I want to be Fern," Jennifer crooned, "and have a pig like Wilbur, and a spider that spins words in her web to save her friend from being killed." We were so proud of Wilbur and Charlotte when Wilbur won the special prize at the county fair and thus was spared from ending up as smoked bacon and ham. We were two chapters from the end when . . . Jennifer spent an afternoon at my friend Laurie's house.

I knew something was wrong when I picked her up. Jennifer hadn't been crying, but I could tell she was about to. "Did something happen, sweetheart?"

Silence.

"Did you fall off the climbing structure?"

Silence.

I called Laurie when we got home. "Jennifer and Courtney played really well together," she reported. "They spent a lot of time outside, then watched a video while they had a snack. She was pretty quiet after that, but I thought she was just tired."

Still, Jennifer was mute. I felt her forehead; it was cool. "Hmmm. Do you want to play a game?" I asked.

She nodded her head a little. (At least I was getting some response.) Allison, paying close attention to all of this, toddled off to pull "Chutes and Ladders" out of the cupboard.

The tears came in sobs when Jennifer hit one of those humongous chutes that sent her sliding back to the bottom of the board. "Charlotte died!" she cried. "She died in the video I saw at Courtney's house. She dies, Mom. She dies at the end of the book."

I took a deep breath and drew my hysterical child into my arms. "So that's what's been bothering you. You saw the Charlotte's Web video?" Uh-oh, I thought. "But doesn't she have lots of baby spiders?"

"That doesn't matter," she sobbed.

"Would you like to stop the game now and read the ending together?"

"No!" was her immediate and emphatic response. "I don't ever want to finish that book."

Suddenly I remembered being four years old and in a darkened movie theater, crying uncontrollably when Bambi's mother was shot and killed. I was so traumatized that I closed my eyes during the fire and didn't open them until the movie was over. And I haven't seen *Bambi* ever again.

Jennifer also has remained true to her word. It's been more than eight years, but she has yet to read the final two chapters of *Charlotte's Web*. "Never!" she says.

Boy, did I learn a lesson from that painful experience. Even the greatest book in the library may not be right for every child. Jennifer has been a protector of animals since she was three years old; she gave up eating meat all on her own when she found out where it came from. She is extremely sensitive about animals dying. If I had read the book through to the end on my own (believe it or not, I hadn't), I might have been able to prepare her for the ending. It's too bad she was left with such a miserable impression about *Charlotte*, because, while it is a book about death, it's also a book about friendship. It is a story that her sister vegetarians Allison and Molly, albeit at ages older than four, were able to appreciate through to the very end. They were sad when Charlotte died, but their emotional attachment to Charlotte, Wilbur, and the young Fern added to their enjoyment of the book. Different kids have different reactions.

I waited several months before attempting to tackle another chapter book, which turned out to be Roald Dahl's enormously popular *Charlie and the Chocolate Factory*. Jennifer thought the story about Charlie winning a coveted ticket out of poverty to tour Willy Wonka's chocolate factory was wonderful, but I found the quirky adult characters, especially the four grandparents who live in the same bed, annoyingly unpleasant. Also, the other kids on the tour are downright despicable. "This is weird, Jennifer," I decided. "But I'm glad you're enjoying it." Her kindergarten teacher happened to be a Roald Dahl fan, so Jennifer was able to listen to *James and the Giant Peach*, where the boy James escapes from his mean aunts by flying away in a peach, as a read-aloud in school. Once she was able to read Dahl books to herself, she read them all. Her other favorites are *The Witches*, *Boy*, *The BFG*, and *Matilda*. Allison and I read *Matilda* together before seeing the movie. Though also populated by peculiar and mean adults — along with one especially sweet teacher — I didn't find *Matilda* repulsive, as I did *Charlie*.

So, if *Charlotte* and *Charlie* were less than total successes, what books have worked well as read-alouds for the kids and me? (Note: many of these are the first in a series, or are written by authors who have published several outstanding books for children.)

◆ *Ginger Pye* by Eleanor Estes. This story of a kid-napped dog takes at least a couple of weeks to finish. It's also rather old-fashioned, changes point of view from the kids to the dog then back to the kids again, and frequently digresses from the main story. But oh, it is a funny and absorbing tale that makes for an entertaining and satisfying read-aloud for the entire family.

◆ *The Boggart* by Susan Cooper. This is a book that has kids begging to hear the next chapter about the ancient, mischievous Scottish spirit that mistakenly ends up in downtown Toronto. Yet isn't delayed gratification one of the important skills children acquire from hearing books in installments? "Sorry, guys," I say. "Gotta wait until tomorrow night to find out what happens." (That is, unless one of my children spirits the book off to bed with her.) I saved the sequel, *The Boggart and the Monster*, to read every night in our hotel room during a week's vacation. We felt as if we were reading about an old and beloved friend. "Keep going," Jennifer pleaded at the end of every chapter. Sometimes I did, but sometimes I didn't continue (depending on how tired Molly and Allison were). We finished it, totally satisfied, the night before our plane ride home. *The Boggart and the Monster* remains one of the highlights of an already memorable holiday.

* *Winnie-the-Pooh* and *The House at Pooh Corner* by A. A. Milne. Sure, my kids saw the videos first, but the original stories and illustrations kept us chuckling through both volumes and wondering aloud chapter after chapter, "How could Disney have left *that* out of the movie?"

* *Ace: The Very Important Pig* by Dick King-Smith. Ace, a most clever pig who understands English and grunts twice for yes and once for no, is the great-grandson of another King-Smith animal hero, Babe, of *Babe: The Gallant Pig* (the book and the movie). Both novels are delightfully clever. We believe these pigs can do what they say they can do. *Ace* is a safer bet, however, for children who are sensitive to animals and death (Jennifer did *not* like it when Ma the sheep died in *Babe*).

* *Henry Huggins* and *Ribsy* by Beverly Cleary. These books are perfect introductions to Cleary's cast of endearing characters who live on Klickitat Street in the "Henry" and "Ramona" books.

* *All About Sam* by Lois Lowry. Sam inspires giggles all around as he describes his first few years as the youngest member of the Krupnik family.

* *The Wonderful Flight to the Mushroom Planet* by Eleanor Cameron and *Rusty's Space Ship* by Evelyn Sibley Lampman. It's amazing, but books about what people in the '50s thought space travel would be like continue to appeal to children for whom a space shuttle takeoff is nothing more than a sound bite on the nightly news. Kids take flight in these exciting books that make terrific read-alouds for all ages.

* *Do You Know Me* by Nancy Farmer. This is a witty and at the same time thought-provoking book about a girl from a contemporary middle-class African family and the adventures she has with her not-at-all-cosmopolitan uncle. It's only ten chapters long, so it is easily finished in a week or so. Jennifer, however, was so eager to know how it ended that she just *had* to read the last chapter to herself — even though it was

9:30 p.m. and she had to get up early the next morning for third grade.

* *Homer Price* by Robert McCloskey. Uncle Ulysses' doughnut machine fiasco and the way in which the clever Miss Terwilliger wins the string-saving contests are our favorite stories from this treasure.

* *The Golden Compass* by Philip Pullman. My friend Catherine and her children, Leah and Josh, consider this fantasy adventure set in a parallel universe and starring a gutsy young girl named Lyra their all-time favorite family read-aloud. "It has the wonderful breadth and complexity of an epic tale," Catherine e-mailed from Pennsylvania. "It's fairly academic in the opening chapters, but after the first child was kidnapped, the book had the full attention of my almost ten- and almost twelve-year-olds. We could hardly wait to get to our read-aloud time every night, which is not an easy feat with the amount of homework that fifth and sixth graders have to undertake." Fortunately, the second part of Philip Pullman's *His Dark Materials* trilogy, *The Subtle Knife*, came out the following summer, so nightly reading didn't have to compete with daily homework assignments.

Many families I know enjoy delving nightly into the classic series books or story collections. These books are excellent for vocabulary enhancement. Remember, a child's listening level is higher than her reading level, and even young children will enjoy many of following: "The Chronicles of Narnia," usually beginning with *The Lion, the Witch and the Wardrobe*; the "Oz" books; the "Little House" books, which start with *Little House in the Big Woods*; *Little Women* and *Little Men*; *The Tale of Peter Rabbit*; *Alice's Adventures in Wonderland* and *Through the Looking Glass*; *Grimm's Fairy Tales*; *Just So Stories* and *The Jungle Books*; *Treasure Island* and *Kidnapped*; *The Hobbit*; *Mary Poppins*; *Peter Pan*; *The Secret Garden* and *The Little Princess*; *The Wind in the Willows*; *Tom Sawyer* and *Huckleberry Finn*; *A Wrinkle in Time*; and *A Christmas Carol*. Brian Jacques's "Redwall" series, though new, is on its way to becoming a classic family favorite read-aloud.

Older children whose parents are persistent in reading to them can benefit from hearing and then talking about a book that brings up sometimes disturbing or profound questions. *Tuck Everlasting*, *The Giver*, and *Baby* are three books I believe parents and children should read together, and not only because they raise difficult issues. These works represent three of the best in modern children's literature. Adults who are smart enough to read them will realize that children's books are *not* just for kids.

In *Tuck Everlasting*, ten-year-old Winnie Foster must decide whether to drink from the fountain of youth she discovers in a spring in the woods. Warning: there is a murder in this book, but even squeamish Jennifer quickly concluded it was justifiable homicide. Winnie's predicament is surprisingly real and the Tuck family wonderfully unforgettable. A couple of laugh-out-loud passages add to the brilliance of Natalie Babbitt's touching story that introduces children to the idea of immortality.

What is utopia? Could it be a society that has eliminated conflict, poverty, hunger, terror, cruelty, and injustice? (Not to mention gender stereotypes?) An existence where everyone knows precisely what to do, how to act and what to say? (Always incredibly politely, of course.) A world without risks? This is the futuristic community envisioned by Lois Lowry in her powerful novel, *The Giver*. Twelve-year-old Jonas is chosen to be the receiver of all the memories that his fellow citizens never knew — war, pain, loneliness, loss, and *feelings*. Also, though — color, love, and real happiness. What he decides to do with his memories, and the knowledge of the lies that exist in a community that has no feelings, is startling and frightening.

Children should know this book, and they should know it with an adult they trust to talk about it with them. The last eight or so chapters of *The Giver* are so riveting that if this is read aloud, plenty of time should be set aside to finish it in one sitting . . . and then to discuss it. (This is also the case with the other book that earned Lois Lowry a Newbery

Award for the most distinguished contribution to American literature for children, *Number the Stars,* a gripping novel of heroism by a ten-year-old girl and her family during the Nazi occupation of Denmark.) *The Giver* is not a book for younger children, however. Save it for those who are at least as old as the fictional Jonas. They will be able to understand and appreciate the story — even the climactic ending.

Patricia MacLachlan's *Baby* is another fine book about feelings and memories. The story begins when an almost year-old baby is left on a family's doorstep. Larkin, her parents, and her grandmother know Sophie's stay is only temporary, yet take her into their hearts as well as their home. By doing so they can't help but remember and begin to talk about their own baby who recently had died at birth. Thought-provoking, yes. Though, like *Tuck Everlasting*, it has moments of levity that help the story remain long in our memories. I cry every time I get to the ending of *Baby*, right there on the family room couch with my children at my side. (Mom has feelings too, I'm not ashamed to admit.)

My favorite children's book to read out loud has to be Nancy Farmer's Newbery Honor Award winner *The Ear, the Eye and the Arm*. Set in Zimbabwe in the year 2194, three children of the country's Chief of Security are kidnapped when they venture for the first time outside the family's guarded compound. Their mother hires mutant detectives Ear, Eye, and Arm to find Tendai, Rita, and Kuda. Before they do (it's incredible when I realize that the two sets of main characters never meet until the final chapters), the children have an amazing series of adventures in remarkable places with extraordinary characters. This is story-telling at its finest. The ending is so exciting, so satisfying, and at the same time so darn funny that my kids have actually hugged the book when I've finished reading it.

Now *that's* a good read-aloud. 🐛

Books

Alcott, Louisa May, *Little Women* (1868); *Little Men* (1871)

Babbitt, Natalie, *Tuck Everlasting* (1975)

Barrie, J. M., *Peter Pan* (1905)

Baum, L. Frank, *The Wonderful Wizard of Oz* (1900)

Burnett, Frances Hodgson, *The Secret Garden* (1911); *A Little Princess* (1905)

Cameron, Eleanor, *The Wonderful Flight to the Mushroom Planet* (1954)

Carroll, Lewis, *Alice's Adventures in Wonderland* (1865); *Through the Looking Glass* (1871)

Cleary, Beverly, *Ribsy* (1964); *Henry Huggins* (1950), both illustrated by Louis Darling

Cooper, Susan, *The Boggart* (1993); *The Boggart and the Monster* (1997)

Dahl, Roald, *Charlie and the Chocolate Factory*, illustrated by Faith Jacques (1964); *The BFG*, illustrated by Quentin Blake (1982); *The Witches*, illustrated by Quentin Blake (1983); *James and the Giant Peach*, illustrated by Emma Chichester Clark (1961); *Boy: Tales of Childhood* (1984); *Matilda*, illustrated by Quentin Blake (1988)

Estes, Eleanor, *Ginger Pye* (1951)

Farmer, Nancy, *Do You Know Me* (1993), illustrated by Shelley Jackson; *The Ear, the Eye and the Arm* (1994)

Grahame, Kenneth, *The Wind in the Willows* (1908)

Jacques, Brian, *Redwall* (1986)

King-Smith, Dick, *Ace: The Very Important Pig*, illustrated by Lynette Hemmant (1990); *Babe: The Gallant Pig*, illustrated by Mary Rayner (1985)

Kipling, Rudyard, *Just So Stories* (1902); *The Jungle Books* (1894)

Lampman, Evelyn Sibley, *Rusty's Space Ship* (1957)

L'Engle, Madeleine, *A Wrinkle in Time* (1963)

Lewis, C. S., *The Lion, the Witch and the Wardrobe* (1950)

Lowry, Lois, *All About Sam*, illustrated by Diane deGroat (1988); *Number the Stars* (1989); *The Giver* (1993)

MacLachlan, Patricia, *Baby* (1993)

McCloskey, Robert, *Homer Price* (1943)

Milne, A. A., *Winnie-the-Pooh* (1926); *The House at Pooh Corner* (1928), both illustrated by Ernest Shepard

Potter, Beatrix, *The Tale of Peter Rabbit* (1902)

Pullman, Philip, *The Golden Compass* (1996); *The Subtle Knife* (1997)

Segal, Lore, editor, translated by Lore Segal and Randall Jarrell, *The Juniper Tree and Other Tales from Grimm*, illustrated by Maurice Sendak (1973)

Stevenson, Robert Louis, *Treasure Island* (1883); *Kidnapped* (1886)

Tolkien, J. R. R., *The Hobbit* (1937)

Travers, P. L., *Mary Poppins*, illustrated by Mary Shepard (1934)

Twain, Mark, *Tom Sawyer* (1876); *Huckleberry Finn* (1884)

White, E. B., *Charlotte's Web*, illustrated by Garth Williams (1952)

Wilder, Laura Ingalls, *Little House in the Big Woods*, illustrated by Garth Williams (1932)

Easy Reader/First Chapter Books

W hen will my child read?" is second only to "When will my baby be toilet trained?" in provoking anxiety and worry among parents. Oh, I've heard about two-year-olds who supposedly can read, just as I know there are some children who are out of diapers at eighteen months. These, of course, are subjective areas. Parents decide how many "mistakes" per day (zero, two, twenty?) their toddler is allowed. And, whether memorized text and good guesses based on visual clues count as "reading." The youngest child I ever witnessed reading entirely new material was Jennifer's friend Hanae, a month before her fifth birthday. Their preschool teacher was sending a letter home to families about the holidays, and before Hanae gave the note to her mother, Cheryl, Hanae sat down on the rug and read every word of the letter out loud. "She can read!" I exclaimed.

"She's been reading for a few months now," Cheryl said. By the time Hanae was five, she was reading very well, but her parents didn't have her skip kindergarten. Jennifer and Hanae went to different elementary schools, but were placed in the same sixth-grade class in middle school. What a happy coincidence. Hanae is still extremely bright; she's one of those kids I made a point to ask what she enjoyed reading over the summer (*Just So Stories*, for one).

Not many children read before starting school. (Children don't really *need* to read before starting school, and I certainly *do* not believe in pushing kids to read prematurely. Surrounded by a rich literary environment, Hanae practically taught herself. That's different.) Not many children are like Rufus Moffat, the five-and-a-half-year-old character in Eleanor Estes's *The Moffats*, who loved the "shiny book" handed out by his teacher the first day of school in about the year 1915. Most children first read books that have been published in the last forty years, called "easy readers" or "first chapter books."

I remember when each of my daughters learned to walk. I recall, as well, which books they were first able to read: Jennifer, *No Tooth, No Quarter!*; Allison, *Last One In Is a Rotten Egg*; Molly, *Ten Apples Up On Top!* Each of these is one of a series of books written and illustrated specifically for beginning readers. Publishers have different names for their series, and sometimes the books have grade levels stamped on them as well. I use these as a guide, but only a guide. Jennifer was dropping teeth out of her mouth right and left when she mastered Jon Buller and Susan Shade's *No Tooth, No Quarter!* the summer before first grade. It's supposedly a book for second and third graders, but her keen interest in teeth and the tooth fairy inspired her to become proficient at a book above her grade level.

Some of the best authors of children's books have written easy readers. Jennifer's friend Leah read, loved, and savored every Arnold Lobel "Frog and Toad" book in the library, beginning with *Frog and Toad are Friends*. This series about two best friends is both easy to read and fun to read. The books have real (albeit short) chapters, which makes beginning readers feel *so* grown up. Another pair of buddies for the easy reader crowd is James Marshall's *George* and Martha, two lovable hippopotamuses that star in seven chapter books (the first of which is titled, simply, *George and Martha*). Molly received the set of four Else Holmelund Minarik and Maurice Sendak's *Little Bear* books for her fourth birthday, so the stories and characters were old friends by the time she could read them out loud to me.

Cynthia Rylant and Suçie Stevenson teamed up to write and illustrate more than a dozen delightful easy readers starring Henry, an only child, and Mudge, his big dog. In the first book, *Henry and Mudge*, Henry picks out his puppy and the two grow to be fast friends — but not before Mudge wanders away from home and becomes (the reader fears) hopelessly lost. Henry's search is successful, thank goodness, and children just know that Mudge will never again leave home without Henry. They usually also want to read another "Henry and Mudge" book. Molly and I can go through six in an hour; when we're finished, we feel all cozy and warm, as if we've just shared a cup of hot chocolate with a friend on a cold winter day.

Humor is an important element in many of these easy readers. Young children love to laugh, and humor keeps them reading and rereading the books. Dr. Seuss books are brimming with humor and charm, as well as goofy pictures and creative and inspiring wordplay. One of Jennifer's vivid memories of learning to read was coming across *Hop on Pop* one afternoon. "I thought it was the funniest thing in the world," she recalls. "And I could read it myself!" Our other Seuss favorites are *The Cat in the Hat* and *Green Eggs and Ham*. A few years ago the girls' Aunt Katie sent the collection *Six by Seuss* for Christmas. I left it out on our coffee table for months. Children and adult visitors alike picked it up to find and giggle over a beloved Seuss title. Publishers continue to look for "the next Dr. Seuss," but I don't think there will ever be another. Theodor Geisel's genius was as unique as it was zany. We should all just be grateful he was so prolific.

One of the funnier characters in books for children learning to read is Peggy Parish's Amelia Bedelia, the maid who takes all of her orders literally and bakes the best lemon-meringue pies. Most kids have never seen a maid (I know that mine haven't), but they know you aren't supposed to dust the furniture with dusting powder, put the lights out on the clothesline, or dress a chicken with clothes. Allison laughs out loud every time she gets to the part in *Merry Christmas, Amelia Bedelia* when Amelia Bedelia (who never, by the way, goes by her first name alone) tries to tie basketballs and footballs onto the Christmas tree.

There are two anthologies of easy readers we have enjoyed immensely: Joanna Cole and Stephanie Calmenson's *Ready . . . Set . . . Read!* and *Ready . . . Set . . . Read —and Laugh!* These books are a great introduction to stories for beginning readers by many of the star authors and illustrators of contemporary children's literature. The collections also include poems, riddles, jokes, and rebuses. A kid can spend hours studying one of these books.

In our town's children's library, easy readers are identified by a yellow dot on the spine; I imagine other libraries use similar coding. In bookstores, there are usually racks of first chapter books. When my daughters have reached the stage where they want to sample as many books as possible in a week, we usually hit the library for a stack of books. Favorites are added to our bookstore shopping list.

There is a wonderfully wide variety of types of easy-to-read books. This is a good time in a child's development, I feel, both to capitalize on her interests by reading many books about a subject she likes, and to help her discover new territories. Here are some of the well-thumbed easy readers I pulled from my children's bookshelves:

- *The Golly Sisters Go West* (Betsy Byars, illustrated by Sue Truesdell); *Danny and the Dinosaur* (Syd Hoff); *Grandmas at Bat* and *Grandmas at the Lake* (Emily Arnold McCully); *Uncle Foster's Hat Tree* (Doug Cushman); *Hazel Saves the Day* (SuAnn Kiser, illustrated by Betsy Day) — humor
- *The Boston Coffee Party* (Doreen Rappaport, illustrated by Emily Arnold McCully) — historical fiction
- *Dinosaur Days* (Joyce Milton, illustrated by Richard Roe) — nonfiction

- *Molly the Brave and Me* (Jane O'Connor, illustrated by Sheila Hamanaka) — realistic fiction/friendship
- *My Brother, Ant* and *Ant Plays Bear* (Betsy Byars, illustrated by Marc Simont) — realistic fiction/sibling relationships
- *Aunt Eater Loves a Mystery* (Doug Cushman) — mystery
- *Surprises* and *More Surprises* (Lee Bennett Hopkins, illustrated by Megan Lloyd) — poetry
- *Little Witch's Big Night* (Deborah Hautzig, illustrated by Marc Brown) — fantasy
- *Grover Learns to Read* (Dan Elliott, illustrated by Normand Chartier) — *Sesame Street* characters

What makes these books popular with kids and parents is that they make reading fun. They have stories or poems that are worth reading, not lists of words put together for the sake of teaching letter sounds. I always watch Molly's eyes go up to the picture when she stumbles on a word. She knows well that the illustrations can give her clues. (Then I jump in and help her sound it out if she still needs help.) Of course it takes more time to listen to my daughter read one of these books all the way through than it does to read it aloud myself, but listening to her is the only way I know if she's really reading. If she gets tired, she knows she can hand the book back to me to finish. And if there is a chronic problem in her reading, I can spot it and bring it up with her teacher. For the most part, though, she makes fewer mistakes every time, which is a treat for both Bill and me to witness.

One step up from easy readers are longer chapter books. The stories are more involved, and while there are still illustrations, they are no longer on every page. Paula Danziger's *Amber Brown is Not a Crayon* is a funny, thoughtful chapter book for children ready to read on their own (and there are sequels, even!). Other favorites in our family include: Mary Pope Osborne's "Magic Tree House" series, beginning with *Dinosaurs Before Dark*; Cynthia Rylant's *The Blue Hill Meadows*; Kathleen Leverich's *Best Enemies*; Dian Curtis

Regan's *The Class with the Summer Birthdays*; Elizabeth Kohler-Pentacoff's *Louise, the One and Only* and *Wish Magic*; and Jackie French Koller's *The Dragonling*. I've also heard that many kids are enjoying Dan Greenburg's goofy "Zack Files" series. The first book, about a reincarnated black sheep (turned cat) of the family, has a wonderful title: *Great-Grandpa's in the Litter Box*. Patricia MacLachlan's *Sarah, Plain and Tall* is considered a chapter book but is such a literary masterpiece that I think it's best saved for a read-aloud so the entire family can enjoy, appreciate, and talk about it. Children can go back to reread it to themselves.

Children who find joy in reading are usually those who find it easy. Easy reader books can help kids take a big step down the path to becoming proficient, independent readers. (And yes, better students as well.) The books also can take the anxiety away from parents who wonder, "When will my child read?" With easy readers, parents know how well their child is doing, and everyone can relax and enjoy the stories along the way. 🍃

Books

Buller, Jon and Susan Shade, *No Tooth, No Quarter!* (1989)

Byars, Betsy, *The Golly Sisters Go West*, illustrated by Sue Truesdell (1985)

Byars, Betsy, *My Brother, Ant* (1996); *Ant Plays Bear* (1997), both illustrated by Marc Simont

Cole, Joanna and Stephanie Calmenson, editors, *Ready . . . Set . . . Read!* (1990); *Ready . . . Set . . . Read—and Laugh!* (1995)

Cushman, Doug, *Aunt Eater Loves a Mystery* (1987); *Uncle Foster's Hat Tree* (1988)

Danziger, Paula, *Amber Brown is Not a Crayon*, illustrated by Tony Ross (1994)

Elliott, Dan, *Grover Learns to Read*, illustrated by Normand Chartier (1985)

Estes, Eleanor, *The Moffats* (1941)

Greenburg, Dan, *Great-Grandpa's in the Litter Box*, illustrated by Jack E. Davis (1996)

Hautzig, Deborah, *Little Witch's Big Night*, illustrated by Marc Brown (1984)

Hoff, Syd, *Danny and the Dinosaur* (1958)

Hopkins, Lee Bennett, selector, *Surprises* (1984); *More Surprises* (1987), both illustrated by Megan Lloyd

Kessler, Leonard, *Last One In Is a Rotten Egg* (1969)

Kiser, SuAnn, *Hazel Saves the Day*, illustrated by Betsy Day (1994)

Kohler-Pentacoff, Elizabeth, *Louise, the One and Only* (1995); *Wish Magic* (1996), both illustrated by R. W. Alley

Koller, Jackie French, *The Dragonling*, illustrated by Judith Mitchell (1990)

LeSieg, Theo., *Ten Apples Up On Top!*, illustrated by Roy McKie (1961)

Leverich, Kathleen, *Best Enemies*, illustrated by Susan Condie Lamb (1989)

Lobel, Arnold, *Frog and Toad are Friends* (1970)

MacLachlan, Patricia, *Sarah, Plain and Tall* (1985)

Marshall, James, *George and Martha* (1972)

McCully, Emily Arnold, *Grandmas at the Lake* (1990); *Grandmas at Bat* (1993)

Milton, Joyce, *Dinosaur Days*, illustrated by Richard Roe (1985)

Minarik, Else Holmelund, *Little Bear*, illustrated by Maurice Sendak (1957)

O'Connor, Jane, *Molly the Brave and Me*, illustrated by Sheila Hamanaka (1990)

Osborne, Mary Pope, *Dinosaurs Before Dark*, illustrated by Sal Murdocca (1992)

Parish, Peggy, *Amelia Bedelia*, illustrated by Fritz Siebel (1963); *Merry Christmas, Amelia Bedelia*, illustrated by Lynn Sweat (1986)

Rappaport, Doreen, *The Boston Coffee Party*, illustrated by Emily Arnold McCully (1988)

Regan, Dian Curtis, *The Class with the Summer Birthdays*, illustrated by Susan Guevara (1991)

Rylant, Cynthia, *Henry and Mudge: The First Book of Their Adventures*, illustrated by Suçie Stevenson (1987)

Rylant, Cynthia, *The Blue Hill Meadows*, illustrated by Ellen Beier

Seuss, Dr., *The Cat in the Hat* (1957); *Green Eggs and Ham* (1960); *Hop on Pop* (1963); *Six by Seuss: A treasury of Dr. Seuss classics* (1991)

Middle-grade Favorites

Children who develop a love for stories and reading typically progress along a continuum that begins with toddler books and nursery rhymes. These are followed by picture books and longer books read aloud to them, then easy readers and first chapter books. It is also common for kids to return to simple picture books when they start reading. Children take great pride in being able to read those very books that only a couple of years earlier could only be deciphered by a grown-up. Sometimes as early as the beginning of second grade, but usually during third grade, kids arrive at a point where they are able to read longer chapter books easily on their own.

However, I always caution parents not to panic if their second or third grader isn't reading. Parents should definitely keep on top of their son's or daughter's progress and continue to make reading aloud part of daily life. But they should not have an anxiety attack, or — worse — give the child an anxiety attack if she's eight or nine years old and isn't reading along with her classmates. I offer three examples:

1) Newbery Medalist and beloved children's author Beverly Cleary has been quite open about the fact that she did not read until a rainy Sunday afternoon when she was in third grade.

2) A neighbor of ours also didn't read until that year in school. He is now an engineering student at Stanford University and doing very well indeed.

3) Jennifer's friend Anna was barely reading in second grade, at the same time her friends Jennifer, Leah, and Erin were devouring book after book. Sometime during third grade Anna's reading light clicked on, and when she was in sixth grade and required to count the number of pages she read during the year, the total topped five thousand.

Important note: If you at all suspect that your child has a learning disability, such as dyslexia, you should have him or her evaluated by a professional as soon as possible. I know several extremely intelligent children and adults who would probably have benefited from an earlier diagnosis and intervention.

For many children who love to read, third, fourth, and fifth grades can be the golden years when they turn into voracious readers. During those grades, Jennifer would frequently read in bed late into the night. At nine, to my great surprise, I realized she could read a children's book faster than I. The book was Natalie Babbitt's fantasy tale, *The Search for Delicious*, which we both wanted to read after enjoying Babbitt's *Tuck Everlasting*. My daughter may have been reading more for plot and less for detail, but she followed the story all right. She loved it, as did I.

It was a challenge for me to keep up a ready supply of books, and when I had nothing fresh to offer or she hadn't brought home anything new from the library, she pulled out a book she liked to reread, such as *Return to Howliday Inn*. This is her favorite sequel to the funny and clever story of the Monroe pets as told by the family dog that begins with *Bunnicula*, and continues with *Howliday Inn* and *The Celery Stalks at Midnight*.

Friends were always a good source for recommendations. One day in third grade, Jennifer came home with the news that Erin had given "the best" book report. It was on *Half Magic*, and Jennifer asked if we could "please, please, please" go to the library right away, because she, too, wanted to read about the children who discover a charm that grants half a wish. I remember being extremely grateful that a copy was on the library shelf. Jennifer started the book before dinner, and finished it one or two days later. "I loved it!" she gushed.

Edward Eager, the author of *Half Magic* as well as other clever fantasies about extraordinary things happening to ordinary children, acknowledged the influence of British writer E. Nesbit in his own books. I had heard about Nesbit's *Five Children and It* from an English friend, whose children had relished that book and *The Enchanted Castle* as much as the characters Jane, Katharine, Mark, and Martha do in *Half Magic*.

Fantasies are an extremely popular form of fiction with middle-grade readers, and have been at least since the publication of Lewis Carroll's *Alice's Adventures in Wonderland* in 1865. L. Frank Baum's *The Wonderful Wizard of Oz* (and sequels) takes readers on a multitude of magical adventures. As a child, I also loved P. L. Travers's *Mary Poppins* and J. R. R. Tolkien's *The Hobbit*, as well as Astrid Lindgren's *Pippi Longstocking*. (My kids, unfortunately, saw the *Pippi* video, which is abominable. It's dreadfully dubbed, and Pippi comes across as a brat, not the high spirit she is in the book. Unlike *The Wizard of Oz*, don't see the movie first. Better yet, don't see the *Pippi* movie at all!) C. S. Lewis's "Chronicles of Narnia," particularly the first two books, *The Magician's Nephew* and *The Lion, the Witch and the Wardrobe*, have engaged the imaginations of my girls. Many children I know read all of Susan Cooper's "Dark is Rising" quintet, beginning with *Over Sea, Under Stone*. Kids who like those books should know about Lloyd Alexander's "Chronicles of Prydain," which begins with *The Book of Three*, and Philip Pullman's "His Dark Materials" trilogy, starting with *The Golden Compass*.

Science fiction, too, appeals to kids who think about "what ifs?" My favorite science fiction fantasy for children is Madeleine L'Engle's 1963 Newbery winner, *A Wrinkle in Time*. It begins realistically enough, with Snoopy's favorite opening line: "It was a dark and stormy night." After a few chapters, however, Meg, along with her precocious younger brother Charles Wallace, and their neighbor Calvin, are whisked beyond reality — through space and time with three marvelous characters, Mrs. Whatsit, Mrs. Who, and Mrs. Which, on a quest to rescue the children's research scientist father from the forces of evil. It's a whopper of a ride, as well as a complex, thought-provoking novel that's nearly impossible to put down. Fortunately there are more books about the Murray family, including *A Wind in the Door* and *A Swiftly Tilting Planet*. John Christopher's *The White Mountains* is also popular with boys and girls who like science fiction.

When I considered the books my children were attracted to at this age, I realized that many of them feature a main character who keeps a notebook or journal. Harriet M. Welsch, the inimitable eleven-year-old protagonist of Louise Fitzhugh's classic, *Harriet the Spy*, keeps her notebook with her at all times — until her mother takes it away after Harriet's spying and notebook observations cause a huge blowup with her friends at school. Alas, Harriet's parents and friends don't understand her, but her nanny, Ole Golly, does and loves Harriet for who she is. Ole Golly knows that a good spy stands up for herself and also that Harriet can get along without Ole Golly.

Jennifer read *Harriet the Spy* at least four times. Allison loved the book so much that she came up with her own spy outfit and wore it for Halloween in fourth grade. For some girls, *Harriet* comes close to cult status. Why? I think because Harriet is strong and independent. She's not perfect. She gets into trouble, but figures her way out of it. She's an outcast, and most girls — even the supposedly popular ones

— feel out of it at times. *Harriet* also describes a period not so very long ago when children had more freedom. Parents in 1964 considered the Soviet Union more of a threat than kidnappers. Children were on their own when they weren't in school. I certainly was: not only did I play baseball with my brothers way down the block for hours on end , but my best friend Joyce and I walked or rode our bikes downtown for lunch every Saturday. I've never allowed my daughters that independence from adult supervision. A year or so ago I asked Joyce (who still lives where we grew up) if she let her daughter go downtown for lunch with her friends. "Never," she replied.

"It's sad, isn't it?" we said.

But in *Harriet the Spy*, a young girl is free to devise an after-school spy route that covers no less than the Upper East Side of New York City. She's in control. She's free. And that's appealing to any reader.

Harriet was the second character Allison identified with who kept a notebook. Amelia, the character/author of Marissa Moss's *Amelia's Notebook* (and sequels), records her thoughts and illustrates her observations in those blue-lined composition books with black-and-white speckled covers. It's a clever concept carried out with humor and sensitivity, whether Amelia writes about moving to a new town (in *Amelia's Notebook*) or tells of her fears when an arsonist sets fire to her school (in *Amelia Writes Again*). Even before Moss's *My Notebook (with help from Amelia)* was published, *Amelia* inspired Allison to purchase and write in her own "Top Secret" notebook. I don't know what's in it, and that's fine with both of us.

Obviously not all journal keepers are female, as the main character in Beverly Cleary's touching 1984 Newbery winner, *Dear Mr. Henshaw*, (and the sequel, *Strider*) ably demonstrates. Leigh Botts wants to be a "famous book writer" like his favorite author, Boyd Henshaw. He begins by writing letters, and later, after encouragement from Mr. Henshaw, a diary. Leigh's life isn't easy — his parents are divorced, someone is stealing the best parts of his lunch, and he doesn't have any friends in the town he and his mom just moved to. (How a child reacts to being the new kid in town is a common theme in many middle-grade novels.) Leigh's dad is a truckdriver who's almost always on the road. He rarely calls or sees his son. During six months of letters and diary entries, Leigh comes to accept his father's place in his life. He also rigs up an ingenious alarm system for his lunch box, which earns him respect at school and the beginning of a friendship with a classmate who needs his own personal alarm. Writing in the diary helps Leigh feel better about his life, and it helps him become a better writer. In the end, he wins a prize in a school writing contest and impresses "a real live author" because he wrote about something that was important to him.

The most serious diary published during the 20th century is, of course, Anne Frank's *The Diary of a Young Girl*. Jennifer's friend Leah wrote her first article for her middle school newspaper on this unique book about the girl who wrote to "Kitty," her diary, all about life in hiding from the Nazis during World War II. On a scale of one to ten, Leah gave *The Diary of Anne Frank* a score of ten, "Because reading the story, I became Kitty listening to Anne, and I could feel what it was like for her to enter adolescence. The story is about something that happened a long time ago. But at the same time, it is about each of us today." Well said.

Anne Frank was a real girl who suffered and died because of other people's cruelty. Even in fiction death isn't easy, but reading about it is important for children, I believe. Through stories they can learn along with the characters about grief and compassion. I had heard of Katherine Paterson's 1978 Newbery Award winner, *Bridge to Terabithia*, for years before Jennifer and I read it together. We knew one of the main characters was going to die in this compelling story of friendship, self-acceptance, and the power of imagination. But we allowed ourselves to be pulled in, and we weren't sorry for it. Leslie gave Jess so much in the short time they were friends, and while her accidental death is incredibly sad, Jess is better off for having known Leslie. So are the fortunate readers of *Bridge to Terabithia*. Jess and Leslie's story helps children discover that the world is indeed "huge and terrible and beautiful and very fragile." Young readers also learn how to cope with loss, and that life can go on after a tragedy. This is children's literature at its best.

Jennifer is twelve now, with more demands on her time than ever before — schoolwork, plays, and those socially critical long talks on the phone with friends. Plus, she needs more sleep. If she's working on her homework out where I'm reading to her sisters, she may be able to listen and occasionally pop over to my grandmother's chair for a chapter or two, but if I read to her it's most likely to review what she needs to know for a test the next day. One winter night she looked in on Allison, who was happily reading *The Middle Moffat* in bed. "I haven't read a book for fun in a long time," she complained. We both sighed, and I put my arm around her. The door is closing on Jennifer's middle years. At least she'll have the summer to catch up on free reading. (We hope.) 🐛

Books

Alexander, Lloyd, *The Book of Three* (1964)
Babbitt, Natalie, *The Search for Delicious* (1969); *Tuck Everlasting* (1975)
Baum, L. Frank, *The Wonderful Wizard of Oz* (1900)
Carroll, Lewis, *Alice's Adventures in Wonderland* (1865)
Christopher, John, *The White Mountains* (1967)
Cleary, Beverly, *Dear Mr. Henshaw* (1983); *Strider* (1991), both illustrated by Paul O. Zelinsky
Cooper, Susan, *Over Sea, Under Stone* (1965)
Eager, Edward, *Half Magic* (1954)
Estes, Eleanor, *The Middle Moffat* (1942)
Fitzhugh, Louise, *Harriet the Spy* (1964)
Frank, Anne, *The Diary of a Young Girl* (1952)
Howe, Deborah and James, *Bunnicula: A Rabbit Tale of Mystery*, illustrated by Alan Daniel (1979)
Howe, James, *Howliday Inn*, illustrated by Lynn Munsinger (1982); *The Celery Stalks at Midnight*, illustrated by Leslie Morrill (1983); *Return to Howliday Inn*, illustrated by Alan Daniel (1992)

L'Engle, Madeleine, *A Wrinkle in Time* (1962); *A Wind in the Door* (1973); *A Swiftly Tilting Planet* (1978)

Lewis, C. S., *The Magician's Nephew* (1955); *The Lion, the Witch and the Wardrobe* (1950)

Lindgren, Astrid, *Pippi Longstocking*, illustrated by Louis S. Glanzman (1950)

Moss, Marissa, *Amelia's Notebook* (1995); *Amelia Writes Again* (1996); *My Notebook (with help from Amelia)* (1997); *Amelia Hits the Road* (1997)

Nesbit, E., *Five Children and It* (1902); *The Enchanted Castle* (1907)

Paterson, Katherine, *Bridge to Terabithia* (1977)

Pullman, Philip, *The Golden Compass* (1996)

Tolkien, J. R. R., *The Hobbit* (1938)

Travers, P. L., *Mary Poppins*, illustrated by Mary Shepard (1934)

Favorite Authors
(A Dinner Table Conversation)

Whenever one of my daughters reads a book she likes a lot, she immediately wants to find out if the author has written anything else. Bette Bao Lord (*In the Year of the Boar and Jackie Robinson*) and Norton Juster (*The Phantom Tollbooth*) have but one great children's book to their names, but Lois Lowry, Nancy Farmer, and Dick King-Smith — to name three of our favorites — have published numerous novels that our family has enjoyed through the years.

"Mom," Allison began at the dinner table when I told her I was writing about our favorite authors, "I know you don't like Roald Dahl, but I loved *Matilda* and *The Witches*, and *James and the Giant Peach*."

"*Boy*," Jennifer added. "It's his autobiography. It's really cool. So is *The BFG*."

"Who, or what, is the BFG?" Bill asked.

"The Big Friendly Giant, Dad," Jennifer explained. "He's one of Roald Dahl's best characters."

"How about Beverly Cleary?" Allison asked. "I loved *Ribsy* and the books about Ramona."

"And of course *Dear Mr. Henshaw*," Jennifer said. "What about Judy Blume? The Fudge books and *Are You There God? It's Me, Margaret*."

"I liked the Fudge books, too," Allison agreed.

Molly looked up from her stuffed baked potato. "Are the Sam books the same as the Fudge books?" she asked.

"No, sweetie," I said. "Lois Lowry wrote those wonderful stories about Sam Krupnik."

"Don't forget Anastasia," Jennifer added. "I've read all the books about her. The one I liked best was the one where she responds to a Personals ad and the guy turns out to be about thirty. She's thirteen."

"*Anastasia at This Address?*" I asked.

"That's it."

"When can I read the Anastasia books?" Allison wondered.

"Any time you want," I said. "You're almost ten, and that's how old Anastasia is in the first one, *Anastasia Krupnik.*"

"She's older in the others, though," Jennifer said.

I smiled at my twelve-year-old. "Yes, Lois Lowry told a group of us at the conference last summer that she loves to *write* about thirteens, not *live* with them."

Jennifer scowled. "Very funny, Mom."

"May I have more milk?" Molly asked.

"May I have more milk, what, Molly?" Bill replied.

"Please?" Molly corrected herself.

"Of course," Bill said, standing up from the table. "Let's get back to helping Mom with favorite authors. Who can think of another one?"

Jennifer was still frowning. "I'm terrible at remembering authors," she said. "I usually just remember books."

"Okay, then," I said. "What about Nancy Farmer's *The Ear, the Eye and the Arm?*"

"Sure, I remember that. It's great. So is her first one, *Do You Know Me.*"

"I loved that book," Allison recalled. "Uncle Zeka was so funny. I liked the part where he tried to drive a car."

"It took about ten years," I said, "for *Matilda, The Indian in the Cupboard,* and *Babe* to be turned into movies. I can't wait to see a movie made out of *The Ear, the Eye and the Arm*. And Nancy Farmer's book about Nhamo, *A Girl Named Disaster*, is positively stunning."

"Speaking of *Babe*," Jennifer said, "Dick King-Smith is obviously one of our favorite authors. You already know I thought *Ace* was better. *The Invisible Dog* was also really good."

"How about Susan Cooper?" Allison asked.

"Yep, she goes on our list," I said.

Allison continued: "I loved *The Boggart*, and then you read *The Boggart and the Monster* to us on vacation."

"That was *such a* good book," Jennifer said. "I reread it on the plane home, and found all the foreshadowing."

"Susan Cooper is among the best, that's for sure," I said.

"Who wrote *Thirteen Going on Seven?*" Jennifer asked. "That's one I used to read over and over all the time before I got *A Fate Totally Worse than Death*."

"Marilyn Sachs," I replied. "She's written many others I think you'd like. And *do* you remember, Jennifer, what Phyllis Reynolds Naylor books you've read?"

"Give me a hint."

"The Alice books."

"I knew that! I loved all those books. By the way, these are really good potatoes, Mom," Jennifer noted. "Much better than the ones we made in home ec last week. Those were nasty."

"Thank you, Jennifer. Your dad did the mixing, I just stuffed 'em. I assume that the boys in your home ec class helped make your 'nasty' potatoes?"

"Yes. But it wasn't their fault, or ours either. The recipe was horrible."

"Returning to the subject," I said, "Allison, who's your favorite author at the moment?"

"Eleanor Estes! The 'Middle Bear' chapter in *The Middle Moffat* is the best: 'There she was without it, and there it was without her.' I laughed so hard the first time I read that part."

"Ha, ha, ha," Jennifer said sarcastically. "I don't get it."

Allison turned to her older sister. "Jane lost her bear head for the Goldilocks play, and it ended up on one of the bedposts on stage. She found it during the performance."

"I never read the Moffat books," Jennifer said. "But I loved *Ginger Pye*."

Molly set her fork down and gave her face a swipe with her napkin. "I'm full. May I be excused?"

"In a moment," I replied. "We've been talking mostly about chapter books, Molly, but do you have any picture book authors you'd like to mention?"

She thought for a moment, then said decidedly, "Marc Brown and Peggy Rathmann."

"And Dr. Seuss!" Jennifer cried.

"Dr. Seuss!" Allison echoed.

"Everybody says Dr. Seuss," Molly announced. "Now can I be excused?"

"In a moment. We're almost finished. Jennifer, any other novelists?"

"Um. Who wrote *Tuck Everlasting?*"

"Good one! Natalie Babbitt. She also wrote all those other great fantasies."

Jennifer was still thinking. "Remember those books that were, like, the Hot and Cold, Up and Down, Spring and Winter?"

"*The Hot and Cold Summer*," Allison told her.

"That's right," Jennifer said. "I liked Bolivia."

Bill was puzzled. "The country?"

"No, Dad. She's a character in the books. Her parents are anthropologists. She's just a girl."

"Jennifer," I said, "you also enjoyed the stories Johanna Hurwitz compiled for *Birthday Surprises*."

"I liked it until I did that awful diorama for a book report in fifth grade."

"Also in fifth grade you read a book by E. L. Konigsburg," I began, "which was . . . "

"*From the Mixed-Up Files of Mrs. Basil E. Frankweiler*," Jennifer finished. "And you're right, I've read a bunch of other books by her. You should too, Allison."

"Mom," Allison asked, "Who wrote *Baby*?"

I sighed at the mention of that short but powerful novel. "Patricia MacLachlan. She's certainly one of our family's favorite authors."

Molly stood up. "Now can I please be excused?"

My youngest child has had to be so patient. "Yes, you may be excused, Molly," I said, smiling.

"What about my favorite author?" Bill asked.

"Who?" we all replied.

"Scott Adams. He writes *Dilbert*!"

Jennifer stood up excitedly. "*Calvin and Hobbes*!" she cried, waving her fork.

"I'm clearing my dishes," Allison announced. "I've got homework to do."

"And I have a chapter to write," I said. "Thank you, everyone, for your help!" 🍎

Books

Babbitt, Natalie, *Tuck Everlasting* (1975)

Banks, Lynne Reid, *The Indian in the Cupboard*, illustrated by Brock Cole (1981)

Blume, Judy, *Are You There God? It's Me, Margaret* (1970); *Tales of a Fourth Grade Nothing*, illustrated by Roy Doty (1972); *Superfudge* (1980); *Fudge-a-Mania* (1990)

Brown, Marc, *Arthur's Tooth* (1985); *Arthur's Family Vacation* (1993)

Cleary, Beverly, *Beezus and Ramona* (1955); *Ribsy* (1964); *Ramona the Pest* (1968), all illustrated by Louis Darling

Cleary, Beverly, *Ramona the Brave* (1975); *Ramona and Her Father*, (1977); *Ramona and Her Mother* (1979); *Ramona Quimby, Age 8* (1981); *Ramona Forever* (1984), all illustrated by Alan Tiegreen

Cleary, Beverly, *Dear Mr. Henshaw* (1983), illustrated by Paul O. Zelinsky (1983)

Cooper, Susan, *The Boggart* (1993); *The Boggart and the Monster* (1997)

Dahl, Roald, *The BFG*, illustrated by Quentin Blake (1982); *The Witches*, illustrated by Quentin Blake (1983); *James and the Giant Peach*, illustrated by Emma Chichester Clark (1961); *Boy: Tales of Childhood* (1984); *Matilda*, illustrated by Quentin Blake (1988)

Estes, Eleanor, *The Middle Moffat* (1942); *Ginger Pye* (1951)

Farmer, Nancy, *The Ear, the Eye and the Arm* (1994); *Do You Know Me*, illustrated by Shelley Jackson (1993); *The Warm Place* (1994); *A Girl Named Disaster* (1996)

Fleischman, Paul, *A Fate Totally Worse than Death* (1995)

Hurwitz, Johanna, *The Hot and Cold Summer* (1984); *The Cold and Hot Winter* (1988); *The Up and Down Spring* (1993); *The Down and Up Fall* (1996), all illustrated by Gail Owens; editor, *Birthday Surprises: Ten Great Stories to Unwrap* (1995)

Juster, Norton, *The Phantom Tollbooth*, illustrated by Jules Feiffer (1961)

King-Smith, Dick, *Babe: The Gallant Pig*, illustrated by Mary Rayner (1985); *Ace: The Very Important Pig*, illustrated by Lynette Hemmant (1990); *The Invisible Dog*, illustrated by Roger Roth (1993)

Konigsburg, E. L., *From the Mixed-Up Files of Mrs. Basil E. Frankweiler* (1967)

Lord, Bette Bao, *In the Year of the Boar and Jackie Robinson*, illustrated by Marc Simont (1984)

Lowry, Lois, *All About Sam* (1988); *Attaboy, Sam!* (1992); *See You Around, Sam!* (1996), all illustrated by Diane deGroat; *Anastasia Krupnik* (1979); *Anastasia Again!* (1981); *Anastasia at Your Service* (1982); *Anastasia, Ask Your Analyst* (1984); *Anastasia on Her Own* (1985); *Anastasia Has the Answers* (1986) *Anastasia's Chosen Career* (1987); *Anastasia at This Address* (1991); *Anastasia, Absolutely* (1995)

MacLachlan, Patricia, *Baby* (1993)

Naylor, Phyllis Reynolds, *The Agony of Alice* (1985); *Alice in Rapture, Sort of* (1989); *Reluctantly Alice* (1991); *All but Alice* (1992); *Alice in April* (1993); *Alice In-Between* (1994); *Alice the Brave* (1995); *Alice in Lace* (1996); *Outrageously Alice* (1997)

Rathmann, Peggy, *Ruby the Copycat* (1991); *Good Night, Gorilla* (1994); *Officer Buckle and Gloria* (1995)

Sachs, Marilyn, *Thirteen Going on Seven* (1993)

Seuss, Dr., *The Cat in the Hat* (1957); *Green Eggs and Ham* (1960)

Watterson, Bill, *Calvin and Hobbes Tenth Anniversary Book* (1995)

Books Even Boys Like

When I told a fifth-grade friend of ours, Sara, that I was writing a chapter about books even boys like, she said, "That shouldn't take you long." Sara, I knew, was talking about the widely accepted notion that boys her age don't read as much as girls. Indeed, most of the boys she is in school with fit the stereotype. Parents often lament that their sons aren't reading enough, or that they've stopped reading for pleasure altogether. I hear it all the time.

Yes, yes, there *are* exceptions. I know of many boys who read like crazy. Allison tells me about a boy in her fourth-grade class who reads during recess, which is something none of my daughters has ever been tempted to do. Recently I received a note from my friend Catherine in Pennsylvania, pleading for more recommendations for her ten-year-old, Josh, who had read almost everything on my list, including the books for twelve and up. I'm keeping my eye out for him.

As a volunteer in our elementary school library for five years, I've noticed that nonfiction is more popular with boys than with girls. Books about sports and sports teams, space, and drawing are hot topics, as are books about the *Titanic* and biographies of sports heroes. Roald Dahl is without a doubt the most popular author of fiction for boys in the upper grades, followed by Gary Paulsen and Bruce Coville. Shel Silverstein is their favorite poet. Brian Jacques's *Redwall* fantasy (and sequels), Jon Scieszka and Lane Smith's wacky "Time Warp Trio" books, and Donald Sobol's "Encyclopedia Brown" books are boys' favorite series books available in the school library. Matt Christopher's books about sports are always popular. Louis Sachar's "Wayside School" books don't stay long on the shelves, and Garfield comic books are a hot commodity.

I also asked several of my friends for lists of their sons' favorite books. Many authors and titles are the same as in my family — E. B. White's *Stuart Little*, Beverly Cleary's "Ramona" books, and anything by Roald Dahl. Yet there were certain books mentioned more often by boys.

Gary Paulsen's *Hatchet* is a riveting adventure story at the top of many boys' lists. The protagonist, thirteen-year-old Brian Robeson, is on the way to visit his divorced father when the pilot of the single-engine plane he is traveling in dies from a sudden heart attack. Brian crash-lands the plane on a lake in the Canadian wilderness, with only a hatchet on his belt. There he spends nearly two months surviving and becoming, as he puts it, "tough in the head." Brian's physical struggle is paralleled by the psychological battle he was dealing with even before the plane crashed — the knowledge that his mother's involvement with another man precipitated his parents' divorce. *Hatchet* is an extraordinarily well-written, gripping novel.

Brian's Winter is the author's companion book to *Hatchet*, written as if Brian had not been rescued before winter began. Fans of the first book have been devouring this one as well. Another Gary Paulsen favorite of Nathan, the fifth-grade son of my friend Randee, is *Dogsong*, the story of a young boy's quest to return to the old ways of his Eskimo ancestors by attempting a long dogsled journey in order to find "his song."

Nathan also considers Jean Craighead George's *My Side of the Mountain* one of his favorite books. Sam Gribley, the main character in this survival story, actually ran away from his home in the city to his great-grandfather's land in the Catskills. Sam " . . . wanted to do something else," and that he does for a year, living in the inside of a tree until his parents find him and decide to build a real house for the family on Sam's mountain. Readers can learn a great deal about nature and how to live off the land from *My Side of the Mountain*, all the while being treated to an enormously readable novel.

My neighbor Jim read *The Sign of the Beaver* to his sons Jamie and Justin. They looked forward to nightly readings of this story by Elizabeth George Speare of a twelve-year-old's survival in the Maine wilderness . Matt, left alone in a log cabin he and his father built when his father returned to Colonial Massachusetts for the rest of their family, has a series of misfortunes until being rescued by a local Indian chief, Saknis. To repay Saknis for his kindness, Matt agrees to teach Saknis's grandson, Attean, to read. Matt reads *Robinson Crusoe* to his reluctant (at first) student, and as they become friends, Attean as well as the women in the Beaver tribe teach Matt how to survive in the forest.

Saknis eventually decides to lead the tribe to new hunting ground, away from what he knows will become a town for white settlers. Matt is tempted by the invitation to join his Indian friends but chooses instead to stay and wait for his family. They do make it to Sam's cabin, a cabin filled with things "the Indians had given him or had taught him how to make for himself." Sam, too, has changed, but he is thrilled to be reunited with his parents and his sister. *The Sign of the Beaver* is a compelling, fascinating tale of survival, acceptance, and personal growth based on a true story of a boy left alone in Colonial Maine.

My nephew Brian's favorite book when he was eleven was also a historical novel, *Shades of Gray*, by Carolyn Reeder. (I had taken a chance at Christmas that Brian might share his father's fascination with the Civil War.) *Shades of Gray* tells the story of a twelve-year-old Virginian, Will Page, orphaned by the end of the War and sent to live with his mother's sister and her husband, who had refused to join the Confederate cause. Will considers his uncle a traitor, and misses his life of relative comfort in the city. He works hard on the farm, though, and learns after months of observing the family's generosity — including taking in a wounded Union soldier — that "people have to decide for themselves what is right and then stand up for what they believe in." Will realizes that he really does belong on the farm with his aunt, uncle, and spirited cousin. Readers come away from the book understanding that, especially in times of war, there are many different ways to show courage. It may even be expressed in shades of gray. (What a great title!)

Time for Andrew: A Ghost Story by Mary Downing Hahn is an extremely popular book with fifth-grade boys at our school. One friend told me that her son read the book straight through, "without even stopping." (So did I, as a matter of fact.) In *Time for Andrew*, twelve-year-old Drew is sent to Missouri to spend the summer with his great-aunt. Up in the attic of the family's ancestral home, he finds a bag of marbles stashed away by his great-great-uncle, Andrew, as well as an old photo of the boy. As Aunt Blythe tells Drew, "You share a face and a name with a boy who died years before you were born." Or did he die?

Later that night the boy Andrew appears, deathly ill with diphtheria. In an attempt to save Andrew by letting him be treated by modern medicines, Drew switches places with Andrew. He ends up spending his summer in the year 1910, becoming more and more like his uncle as the weeks go by. Making matters interesting for Drew are a loving, budding feminist sister, Hannah, and a bully cousin (Drew's great-grandfather, as a boy). Not only that, he and the real Andrew — who also has to make adjustments in order to fit into a different era — have nightly marble games in the attic. *Time for Andrew* is a real page-turner up to the rewarding, satisfying ending. No wonder boys tell their friends about this book!

Jamie, my young friend who recommended *The Sign of the Beaver*, was reading primarily mega-series books in third and fourth grade until his mom, Terrie, discovered Bill Brittain's *Wings* in our local bookstore. Ian Carras is another twelve-year-old boy faced with a life crisis: he, ah, sprouted wings. This is a complication for Ian's family, especially his father, who, as Ian explains to his friend, "wants to be mayor so bad, he gets the cold sweats just thinking about it." Mr. Carras is annoyed that his son has turned into a "freak," and that the entire family is being hounded by the media. Ian takes refuge with another outcast and her mother at their cabin in the mountains, where he has time to think about what it means to be different — and to try out his new wings. This is an engaging and convincing story. We borrowed Jamie's copy of *Wings*, and Jennifer read it in one sitting. "Good book," she announced.

A librarian friend told me about another chapter book that appeals both to boys and to girls: *The Trading Game* by Alfred Slote. It's about baseball and baseball cards, and friendship and family. Unlike many baseball books, one of the main characters in this book is a girl. (I appreciate that.) *The Trading Game* is a book I always recommend to third- and fourth-grade boys who like baseball, but don't think they like reading. Alfred Slote has also written other sports stories worth checking out. My friend Karen and her son consider *Hang Tough, Paul Mather* "incredible." It's a sensitive novel about a twelve-year-old with leukemia who is determined to pitch the way he did before he became ill, and be part of a winning team from his wheelchair. (Readers of *Hang Tough* should know that the prognosis for children with leukemia is more favorable now than it was in 1973, when the book was published.)

As I was writing this and other chapters, on his own Josh found (and read) two superlative novels he would recommend to *anyone*: *The Glory Field* by Walter Dean Myers, the impressive intergenerational story of an African-American family over 240 years; and *The Thief* by Megan Whalen Turner, a clever tale of suspense and intrigue set in a mythical land much like Greece. Advice taken, I bought *The Glory Field* and *The Thief* for my girls to read.

All these books tell a good story, and a good story is the best enticement I know of to keep the joy of reading fiction alive for boys. As a bonus, these books encourage boys to think, wonder, and feel as they read about the challenges the characters face as their stories unfold. 🍎

Books

Brittain, Bill, *Wings* (1991)

Cleary, Beverly, *Beezus and Ramona* (1955); *Ramona the Pest* (1968), both illustrated by Louis Darling

Cleary, Beverly, *Ramona the Brave* (1975); *Ramona and Her Father*, (1977); *Ramona and Her Mother* (1979); *Ramona Quimby, Age 8* (1981); *Ramona Forever* (1984), all illustrated by Alan Tiegreen

Coville, Bruce, *Jeremy Thatcher, Dragon Hatcher*, Gary A. Lippincott (1991); *Jennifer Murdley's Toad : A Magic Shop Book*, illustrated by Gary A. Lippincott (1992); *My Teacher is an Alien*, illustrated by Mike Wimmer (1989); *Aliens Ate My Homework*, illustrated by Katherine Coville (1993)

George, Jean Craighead, *My Side of the Mountain* (1959)

Hahn, Mary Downing, *Time for Andrew: A Ghost Story* (1994)

Jacques, Brian, *Redwall* (1986); *Mossflower* (1988); *Mattimeo* (1989); *Mariel of Redwall* (1991); *Salamandastron* (1993); *Martin the Warrior* (1994); *The Bellmaker* (1995); *Outcast of Redwall* (1996); *Pearls of Lutra* (1997)

Myers, Walter Dean, *The Glory Field* (1994)

Paulsen, Gary, *Hatchet* (1987); *Brian's Winter* (1996); *Dogsong* (1985)

Reeder, Carolyn, *Shades of Gray* (1989)

Sachar, Louis, *Sideways Stories from Wayside School*, illustrated by Julie Brinckloe (1978); *Wayside School is Falling Down*, illustrated by Joel Schick (1989); *Wayside School Gets a Little Stranger*, illustrated by Joel Schick (1995)

Scieszka, Jon, *Knights of the Kitchen Table* (1991); *The Not-So-Jolly Roger* (1991); *The Good, the Bad, and the Goofy* (1992); *Your Mother Was a Neanderthal* (1993); *2095* (1995); *Tut, Tut* (1996), all illustrated by Lane Smith

Slote, Alfred, *The Trading Game* (1990); *Hang Tough, Paul Mather* (1973)

Sobol, Donald J., *Encyclopedia Brown: Boy Detective*, (1963); *Encyclopedia Brown Finds the Clues* (1966); *Encyclopedia Brown Saves the Day* (1970), all illustrated by Leonard Shortall

Speare, Elizabeth George, *The Sign of the Beaver* (1983)

Turner, Megan Whalen, *The Thief* (1996)

White, E. B., *Stuart Little*, illustrated by Garth Williams (1945)

Series Books

Series books are often an important, transitory component of a child's reading career. When reading independently from Mom and Dad is suddenly possible and children are beginning to pick up speed and comprehension, many kids get addicted to a series and can't wait to read another book about their favorite characters. I was a "Nancy Drew" girl myself, barreling through stories of one mystery after another encountered and solved by the gorgeous, brilliant Nancy and her "chums," Bess and George. My brothers and my husband, not surprisingly, read the "Hardy Boys."

Jennifer ordered her first series book from a school book club at the beginning of second grade. She can still recite the first paragraph of *The Boxcar Children*: "One warm night four children stood in front of a bakery. No one knew them. No one knew where they had come from." Henry, Jessie, Violet, and Benny are orphans who discover an old red boxcar and make it their home. They are soon adopted by their grandfather, and the boxcar takes up residence in the back yard. The kids go on to solve mysteries. This first book about the Alden family took Jennifer a week to finish. By the end of the school year and thirty-two books later, she could read one on a Saturday morning before breakfast. "I always pretended I was Jessie," Jennifer recalled when I asked her and Allison what they remembered about their favorite series.

"I got my whole class reading 'The Boxcar Children' in second grade," Allison said. "We used to have a contest to see who could read the most books. Then Andrew's dad started reading them to him."

"That's not fair!" Jennifer declared.

"As I recall," I said, "Andrew was a first grader that year in your first- and second-grade class. Maybe he just wanted to fit in with the second graders. Series books can be real fads."

"That's the only reason little kids read R. L. Stine," Jennifer said disdainfully.

Ah, yes, "Goosebumps," the best selling children's chapter book series of the 1990s. Some kids — make that a lot of kids — love them. (Other kids just collect "Goosebumps" in numerical order but don't read them.) Most critics agree, though, that they have no literary merit whatsoever. Parents vacillate between the two camps. If R. L. Stine can lure their kids (usually boys) into reading, then they're thrilled. Yet if the parents really sit down and read the books, they may not be so happy. (Let the record show that I don't consider "The Boxcar Children" great literature either.) My friends Terrie and Jim are on the kids' side. Terrie told me once, "We feel like writing R. L. Stine a thank-you note. Jamie's finally reading!"

So I asked Jamie to lend me his favorite book. It was *It Came from Beneath the Sink!* ("He's read it about twelve times," Terrie reported.) I loved the title and I really tried to have an open mind, but . . . even dismissing the grotesque and unimaginative so-called terror in every chapter, the book was so startlingly stupid, humorless, thoughtless, flat, predictable, and obviously cranked out in about two weeks that it made me, well, angry. (Authors in my writers group spend at least a year writing, rewriting, and polishing a novel.) I did not, however, tell Jamie I thought his book was a waste of time and money, because all things considered, I agree with his parents. If this is what's getting him to read for pleasure, then I'm all for it. What I did do was to suggest some exciting, well-written books for Jim and Terrie to read with Jamie and his brother Justin. They started with *The Boggart*.

Sometime during fourth grade, Jamie closed the book on his twenty-eighth (or so) "Goosebumps" book. He looked at his mom and said, "R. L. Stine is so obvious!" Thus, Jamie's "Goosebumps" days were over. He figured out *for himself* that he was being manipulated as a reader and started to look for books that might actually surprise him. When he found good literature, he appreciated it all the more because he recognized fine writing. (Jennifer, at the end of her "Boxcar Children" phase, loved to look for typos and plot inconsistencies.)

Most series books have a reading level that is below the target age of the audience, but children often don't know that unless they read other books as well. Another risk in series books, I believe, is if kids never choose to move beyond them. That's why I find series books for older readers, "Fear Street" and "Sweet Valley High," for example, much more objectionable than the books aimed primarily at kids in elementary school.

The "Baby-Sitters Club" books by Ann M. Martin never really caught on with Jennifer's friends, or Allison's either (peer pressure is *so* important to a series' popularity), but these books about a girls' baby-sitting cooperative turned out to be favorites of the third-grade class that followed Allison. I also know that many boys latch onto the "Encyclopedia Brown" books by Donald J. Sobol. My older daughters collected and read many of the books in the "American Girls" series, and enjoyed them for what they were — formulaic stories about girls in different historical periods.

While "American Girl" doll accessories are always on Allison's and Molly's Christmas and birthday wish lists for their grandma, and their "Girl of Today" dolls (the ones where they got to pick out the hair and eye color) play a significant role in their imaginary games, the literary purist in me is troubled that the series of books is part of a mail order marketing empire. I've read several of the "American Girl" books, and *Changes for Molly* is the only one I feel could stand on its own. (*American Girl* magazine, on the other hand, is excellent. One of Jennifer's all-time favorite short stories, "Suzy and Leah," a moving piece of Holocaust literature by well-respected children's author Jane Yolen, appeared in *American Girl* magazine. Jennifer didn't want to lose track of the story, so she cut it out, punched holes in the pages, and put it in its own binder in our library.)

Contrary to public opinion, there are some series books that have a great deal of literary merit, written by children's book authors who respect their young readers. Joanna Cole and Bruce Degen's clever "Magic School Bus" series combines nonfiction with fantasy in order to teach science. "The Kids of the Polk Street School" series by Patricia Reilly Giff is wonderful for kids just learning to read. Paula Danziger's books about Amber Brown, beginning with *Amber Brown is Not a Crayon*, follow the trials and tribulations of that spunky character and her friends and family. The prolific Gary Paulsen wrote the "Culpepper Adventures" series about Dunc and his best friend, Amos, which my friend Randee's son, Nathan, was hooked on in third grade. Beverly Cleary's "Ramona" books have won awards and millions of fans through the years. Jon Scieszka and Lane Smith's "Time Warp Trio" books keep many boys laughing late into the night. Jennifer stayed up late, too, reading Bruce Balan's first two "Cyber.kdz" books about a group of teenagers (and one ten-year-old) who meet on the Internet and solve high-tech mysteries. Lois Lowry's remarkable novels about the Krupnik family, starring Sam and his older sister Anastasia, have incredible kid appeal. Jennifer has also read every book in Phyllis Reynolds Naylor's "Alice" series at least twice. The "Little House" series by Laura Ingalls Wilder is classic children's literature, as is C. S. Lewis's "The Chronicles of Narnia." Brian Jacques's "Redwall" fantasies are enormously popular and worthwhile reading for more proficient readers.

Whether they are mysteries, horror, humor, fantasy, science, or history, series books are a big chunk of the children's book market. Those that catch on do so because they offer familiar characters or situations to young readers who find comfort in predictability, or who may simply want to read what all the other kids are reading. (There *are* worse fads.) Look for the good series, yet don't make fun if your child latches onto a not-so-spectacular offering. (I'd draw the line at reading "Goosebumps" aloud to a five-year-old, however, when there are hundreds of better books to choose from. Too, little kids have been known to have nightmares from hearing them.) Children — or adults, either — should not have to defend their choice of reading material as long as it's legal and age-appropriate. And that includes *It Came from Beneath the Sink!* 🍏

Books

Balan, Bruce, "Cyber.kdz" series
Cleary, Beverly, "Ramona" series
Cole, Joanna, "Magic School Bus" series, illustrated by Bruce Degen
Cooper, Susan, *The Boggart* (1993)
Danziger, Paula, "Amber Brown" series, illustrated by Tony Ross
Dixon, Franklin W. (pseudonym), "Hardy Boys" series
Giff, Patricia Reilly, "The Kids of the Polk Street School" series, illustrated by Blanche Sims
Jacques, Brian, "Redwall" series
Keene, Carolyn (pseudonym), "Nancy Drew" series
Lewis, C. S., "The Chronicles of Narnia" series
Lowry, Lois, "Anastasia" series; "Sam" series, illustrated by Diane deGroat
Martin, Ann M., "Baby-Sitters Club" series
Naylor, Phyllis Reynolds, "Alice" series
Paulsen, Gary, "Culpepper Adventures" series
Scieszka, Jon, "Time Warp Trio" series, illustrated by Lane Smith
Sobol, Donald J., "Encyclopedia Brown" series
Stine, R. L., "Goosebumps" series, including *It Came From Beneath the Sink!* (1995)
Tripp, Valerie, *Changes for Molly*, illustrated by Nick Backes (1988)

Warner, Gertrude Chandler, "The Boxcar Children" series
Wilder, Laura Ingalls, "Little House" series, illustrated by Garth Williams
Yolen, Jane, "Suzy and Leah," illustrated by Hilary Mosberg, *American Girl* Magazine, May/June 1993

Poetry

owned and loved three big, fat books when I was a child: *The World of Pooh (The Complete Winnie-the-Pooh* and *The House at Pooh Corner); The World of Christopher Robin (The Complete When We Were Very Young* and *Now We Are Six);* and *The Golden Treasury of Poetry.* As it turns out, two of these books are poetry collections. (And I always thought fiction was my favorite genre!)

My Pooh books survived our family's six moves up and down California and criss-crossing the U.S., but my favorite poetry anthology, alas, was lost sometime in the '60s or '70s. I hadn't thought of it for decades myself, until I became a parent and recalled hours spent studying the lines of inspiration penned by (among many others) Robert Louis Stevenson, Edgar Allen Poe, and Emily Dickinson, as well as the silly rhyme about the poor old lady who swallowed a fly (among other creatures). I somehow even remembered the name of the anthologist, Louis Untermeyer, when many years ago I looked for this volume in bookstores so my children could enjoy it as I did. Sadly, I learned it was no longer in print.

We still read and enjoyed poetry, of course. I consider *Goodnight Moon* poetry. Nursery rhymes are poetry. Sandra Boynton's board books, especially *The Going to Bed Book,* quickly became family favorites, learned and recited at early ages. So were many of Shirley Hughes's poems; *Rhymes for Annie Rose* is a delight. *Jesse Bear, What Will You Wear?* is written in verse, as are so many irresistible picture books we read over and over when the girls were little — *Sheep in a Jeep*, *Chicka Chicka Boom Boom*, and *Madeline* among them. I still recite poems by A. A. Milne from my old book, *The World of Christopher Robin*. And need I mention Dr. Seuss? (Yes!)

Young children love pictures to illustrate their poems. *Animal Crackers*, a collection of "Pictures, Poems, and Lullabies for the Very Young" includes gorgeous watercolor paintings by Jane Dyer. *My Very First Mother Goose*, another recent addition to poetry for little ones, is joyously illustrated by Rosemary Wells. Both of these books are splendid introductions to poetry and rhyme.

Jennifer's kindergarten teacher used Maurice Sendak's lively poem, "Chicken Soup with Rice" to teach the names of the months (we bought it as a paperback book to keep at home). In first grade, her teacher made each student a member of the Poetry Club. Parents were invited to the final meeting of the year for recitations of poems by Shel Silverstein, Jack Prelutsky, Lee Bennett Hopkins, and other favorites. The students were so proud of themselves! They never would have been able to memorize an entire book, but a poem — several poems, even — was manageable, and fun to learn by heart. Children who spoke English as a second language seemed to speak poetry as their first. I knew they were learning English by memorizing the poems, even if they weren't aware of it. To this day, Jennifer remembers with fondness her first-grade Poetry Club.

Nonsense can give a new twist to a child's outlook on life. Kids in elementary school love to be silly, and their favorite whimsical poets are Jack Prelutsky and Shel Silverstein. Prelutsky's poems are full of humor and insight, and are a joy to read and hear. His final stanzas or lines will often turn the entire poem around. "Listen to this! Listen to this!" Jennifer said while looking for a poem to recite for her sixth-grade class. The three big collections of Jack Prelutsky's poetry, brilliantly illustrated by James Stevenson, are all winners in our family: *The New Kid on the Block, Something Big Has Been Here*, and *A Pizza the Size of the Sun*.

The dust in our school library never has a chance to settle on Shel Silverstein's first two collections, *Where the Sidewalk Ends* and *A Light in the Attic*. These books give poetry and art a good name for any self-respecting boy or girl. "They're funny!" the kids all say about these books. (Silverstein's latest, *Falling Up*, is not quite as childlike or appealing, I'm afraid.) Another favorite author of ours of short, witty poetry is Jeff Moss, one of the original creators of *Sesame Street*. Chris Demarest's comic line drawings are a perfect complement to Moss's poetry in *The Butterfly Jar* and *The Other Side of the Door*. Children who enjoy the poems of Jack Prelutsky, Shel Silverstein, and Jeff Moss would also appreciate being introduced to the father of twentieth century American humorous verse, Ogden Nash. I especially like the poems selected and illustrated by Quentin Blake in the book, *Custard and Company*.

Poetry doesn't have to make children laugh in order for them to be drawn to it. My favorite poem in the anthology I treasured as a child was Edgar Allen Poe's "Annabel Lee." The narrator's childhood friend and first love dies, for heaven's sake, yet the lyrics had magic for me. For years I kept them in my mind. A Canadian artist, Giles Tibo, obviously had a similar attraction, for he illustrated "Annabel Lee" as a picture book. The paintings are exquisite, and I'm delighted to know that the poem lives on for another generation of readers. Yet I hesitated to share the illustrations with my children. When I first knew and loved the poem, I had had only one simple line drawing to inspire the pictures in my mind. (Yes, I have similar misgivings about music videos.) When I found *Annabel Lee* at the bookstore and brought it home, Allison studied the back cover after I read the poem aloud. "It's a dream?" she asked incredulously.

"Not if you don't want it to be," I replied.

Then, naturally, she looked at the pictures. "I still like the poem better," she decided. Allison and I often recite together the first two verses of "Annabel Lee," and Jennifer learned the entire poem for her final class recitation. ("Yes, yes, yes!" I shouted to myself.)

The collections and anthologies of Lee Bennett Hopkins are among our favorite poetry books for young readers. *Good Books, Good Times*, the book that contains the poem "Good Books, Good Times," (which Jennifer still can recite from first grade), is delightful to read aloud. Hopkins also selected the poems for *Surprises*, *More Surprises*, and *Best Friends*, among many others. Terrific, all of them. It was through these books that we discovered another gifted poet, Myra Cohn Livingston. Her own books of poetry sing with beauty and wisdom. My favorite is *Worlds I Know and Other Poems*.

The poems in Marilyn Singer's collection, *All We Needed to Say*, tell a story from the point of view of two girls who have entirely different attitudes about school. Tanya is the well-behaved student; Sophie is constantly getting into trouble. But they're both likable characters and grow to like each other by the end of the book — brought together by their disdain for the unfair yard-duty teacher. "She got that right," Jennifer said about the author, remembering, I knew, the time she was wrongly accused of a petty offense in fourth grade by a ticket-happy lunchtime playground supervisor. I love the way the poems in *All We Needed to Say* are connected. Photos of an urban school add to the richness of this collection. And though the setting is specific — and quite different from our own elementary school in the suburbs — the feelings Tanya and Sophie have are universal.

Joyful Noise: Poems for Two Voices is Paul Fleischman's Newbery Award-winning collection of poems celebrating the insect world. *Joyful Noise* was " . . . written to be read aloud by two readers at once, a duet with one taking the left-hand part, the other taking the right-hand part." Reading these poems is like making music, and there isn't even the danger of singing off-key! Children of all ages (and adults as well) can't help but appreciate and enjoy the rhythm and the words that so beautifully describe the insects around us. What a joy it is to sit next to your child and read these poems together. Our friend Alejandro, now in high school, was inspired in fifth grade to record himself reading one part of *Joyful Noise*. He added the other part when he gave his oral book report to his class. Alejandro's mother, Magdalena, has kept the tape as a record of her son's creativity in what she calls his "little-boy voice."

Once every two or three weeks I check books out for Allison's fourth-grade class when they visit the school library. One day a girl named Ashley handed me a large, worn book with POETRY written in red letters on the cover. "Oh, my gosh!" I cried. "It's my poetry book!"

"No, it's not," Ashley said politely, "It's *my* poetry book. I want to check it out."

"Of course you get it first," I replied, smiling to reassure her I wasn't going to swipe her book. "What I mean is, this is the poetry book I loved as a child, and I hope you like it even half as much as I did. And when you're finished, I'd like to borrow it to share with Allison and her sisters."

So my old friend *The Golden Treasury of Poetry* was there in the library all along. The illustrations seem slightly out-of-date to me now, but the poems still sing. The beauty of the sound of the language in that volume and all the other poetry books we continue to enjoy are a kind of music to accompany our busy lives. 🌱

Books

Bemelmans, Ludwig, *Madeline* (1939)

Boynton, Sandra, *The Going to Bed Book* (1982)

Brown, Margaret Wise, *Goodnight Moon*, illustrated by Clement Hurd (1947)

Carlstrom, Nancy White, *Jesse Bear, What Will You Wear?*, illustrated by Bruce Degen (1986)

Dyer, Jane, *Animal Crackers* (1996)

Fleischman, Paul, *Joyful Noise: Poems for Two Voices*, illustrated by Eric Beddows (1988)

Hopkins, Lee Bennett, selector, *Good Books, Good Times*, illustrated by Harvey Stevenson (1990)

Hopkins, Lee Bennett, selector, *Best Friends*, illustrated by James Watts (1986)

Hopkins, Lee Bennett, selector, *Surprises* (1984); *More Surprises* (1987), both illustrated by Megan Lloyd

Hughes, Shirley, *Rhymes for Annie Rose* (1995)

Livingston, Myra Cohn, *Worlds I Know and Other Poems*, illustrated by Tim Arnold (1985)

Martin, Bill, Jr. and John Archambault, *Chicka Chicka Boom Boom*, illustrated by Lois Ehlert (1989)

Milne, A. A., *The World of Pooh* (1957); *The World of Christopher Robin* (1958), both illustrated by Ernest Shepard

Moss, Jeff, *The Butterfly Jar* (1989); *The Other Side of the Door* (1991), both illustrated by Chris Demarest

Nash, Ogden, *Custard and Company*, illustrated by Quentin Blake (1980)

Opie, Iona, editor, *My Very First Mother Goose*, illustrated by Rosemary Wells (1996)

Poe, Edgar Allen, *Annabel Lee*, illustrated by Giles Tibo (1987)

Prelutsky, Jack, *The New Kid on the Block* (1984); *Something Big Has Been Here* (1990); *A Pizza the Size of the Sun* (1996), all illustrated by James Stevenson

Sendak, Maurice, *Chicken Soup With Rice* (1962)

Seuss, Dr., *Green Eggs and Ham* (1960)

Shaw, Nancy, *Sheep in a Jeep*, illustrated by Margot Apple (1986)

Silverstein, Shel, *Where the Sidewalk Ends* (1974); *A Light in the Attic* (1981); *Falling Up* (1996)

Singer, Marilyn, *All We Needed to Say*, photographs by Lorna Clark (1996)

Untermeyer, Louis, editor, *The Golden Treasury of Poetry*, illustrated by Joan Walsh Anglund (1959)

Books that Make Us Laugh

I'll never forget the day I brought home *Martha Speaks*, Susan Meddaugh's fabulously funny picture book about Martha the dog. Martha, you see, is able to talk because whenever she eats alphabet soup, the letters go up to her brain instead of down to her stomach. I read *Martha Speaks* at the dinner table that night, and even Bill laughed so hard he nearly fell out of his chair. "Why didn't I write that?" he asked, still giggling. (My husband is known for his quick wit.)

"I wish you had," I said. "It's the funniest book I've read in a long time, and I know kids are going to love it."

"We already do, Mom," six-year-old Allison piped up.

"Yeah, Mom," Jennifer added. "Could you read it again? Now?"

I began again, not stopping until the end, when the police officer tells Martha's family that "Some lady named Martha" called the station to report a robbery, and so the burglar is caught and all's well. We've read *Martha Speaks* hundreds of times since that evening, and bought several copies for birthday presents. The book went on to win several awards, including a *New York Times* Best Illustrated Book. The first sequel, *Martha Calling*, has Martha winning a call-in radio contest (Martha *loves* to talk on the telephone) for her family at an inn where the rule is "No Dogs Allowed." Not for long! It's a delightful book, but *Martha Blah Blah* is even better. Martha is suddenly deprived of half her letters when the greedy new owner of Granny's Soup Company fires thirteen "alphabeticians," and Martha's words are gone (except in footnotes). Plus, Alf the "A" maker, among others, is out of a job. A dejected Martha wanders away, wondering if her family will love her now that she is speechless. We know they love her for who she is, not for what she can do (what a great message!), but she doesn't find that out until Alf shares his last can of *real* alphabet soup with her, and Martha cleverly convinces the new Granny to put the letters back in the soup where they belong. *Martha Blah Blah* is remarkable for making readers and listeners laugh out loud and think about concepts such as corporate downsizing and unconditional love.

I can come up with several other humorous books (or books with funny passages) that make me remember exactly where I was when I first read them. *Flat Stanley* by Jeff Brown was a school book club find when Jennifer was in second grade. That fall we were living temporarily in a four-story townhouse on a street called Ryan Court while our home was being remodeled. I had taken advantage of a cozy spot at the very top of the stairs, outside the bedrooms, as the ideal location for a magazine-style wooden bookrack I had recently purchased. We hadn't carted all of our children's books to Ryan Court, so when Jennifer's book order arrived, I set the paperbacks out on the shelves for the girls to choose from for our nightly reading, which took place on the comfortable carpeted landing.

One evening Jennifer picked out *Flat Stanley*, and we were treated to a wild and witty book based on the premise that a boy named Stanley is flattened by his own bulletin board. At first Stanley enjoys being half an inch thick — he can slide under doors, rescue his mother's ring from beneath the grate in the street, and get to California for the price of an airmail stamp. This makes Stanley's brother jealous; he lets Stanley-the-kite get tangled up in a tree. The story continues with Stanley posing as a sheep girl in a painting to catch a couple of "sneak thieves" who had been stealing paintings from the Famous Museum of Art (headed by Stanley's neighbor, Mr. O. Jay Dart). For a while Stanley is famous himself, yet when kids start making fun of him for being flat, his brother comes up with an ingenious way to make Stanley "round" again.

Flat Stanley is a lot longer than the average picture book. When I first read it, Molly was two years old and *Brown Bear, Brown Bear, What Do You See?* was her favorite bedtime book. Still, she sat through an entire reading of *Flat Stanley* with her older sisters, who laughed with me on nearly every page at the outlandish situation, comical dialogue, and numerous plays on words. Molly didn't get all the jokes (Jennifer and Allison probably didn't get all of them either), but everyone agreed it was a *very* funny book. "Can you read it again, Mom?" Jennifer pleaded.

The story had taken us past Molly's bedtime so I had to say, "Tomorrow night." I returned it to the shelf, which, because of *Flat Stanley*, soon became known as the "favorite books shelf." Molly added *Brown Bear* to it, and for four months we enjoyed our family read-aloud time in front of the favorite books shelf on the landing of our Ryan Court house.

I had the pleasure of hearing Louis Sachar talk at a writers conference one summer about "Writing the Humorous Novel." He began by reading a chapter from *Wayside School Gets a Little Stranger*, the latest in a line of funny books about the thirty-story school (with no nineteenth floor) where the strangest things happen. His "Poetry" chapter had four hundred adults — writers and editors — laughing so loudly in the hotel ballroom that he had to stop several times until we quieted down so we could hear him. I still chuckle when I read the chapter, and Jennifer loves the entire book.

The reviews for Christopher Paul Curtis's stunning first novel, *The Watsons Go to Birmingham — 1963*, were so phenomenal that I bought the book as soon as it was available at my favorite children's bookstore. I began reading it that night while Jennifer finished her fifth-grade geography homework at the kitchen table across from me. I only had to read to page twelve before I started giggling. Soon, tears were streaming down my cheeks. "What *is* so funny, Mom?" Jennifer asked, obviously annoyed.

"This book is a riot! The main character's older brother just got his lips frozen to the outside mirror of the family car. Their mom is running around trying to figure out how to get him unstuck, and the dad can't stop laughing and teasing. Oh, Jennifer, I can't wait until you have time to read this book."

"Calm down, Mom, it's just a book."

But *The Watsons Go to Birmingham* is not just any book. What begins as a side-splitting portrait of a loving, goofy African-American family living in Flint, Michigan, concludes with the ten-year-old protagonist witnessing a racial bombing in Alabama and nearly going crazy because of it. Powerful. The book was noted for its humor as well as its compelling nature when it won a Newbery Honor.

Andrew Clements is another author whose first novel received rave reviews and great word-of-mouth recommendations. One evening I sat down to read *Frindle* after tucking Allison and Molly in, while waiting for Jennifer's car pool to drop her off after a late weeknight performance of *Snow White*. I can't remember ever spending a better hour with a children's book (*Frindle* is only a little over one hundred pages). Its plot involves a fifth-grade boy making up a new word for pen, "frindle," and what happens as the word takes on a life of its own. When Jennifer straggled in at 10:15 — exhausted, sniffly with a cold, and still wearing her stage makeup — she found me chuckling in my grandmother's easy chair. "Jennifer, you have to read this book!" I cried at the ending, and vowed to have everyone in my family read *Frindle* within the week. They did (we read it to Molly), and adored it as much as I did. It's one of those rare books that is literally for all ages.

Like Mary Poppins's Uncle Albert, I love to laugh. It's good for my soul. Though I can't make up jokes (I can't even *remember* more than one joke at a time), I appreciate humor, and I want my children to as well. So I look for humor in books. There are certain picture books that make us laugh every time we read them:

♦ *"Never Spit on Your Shoes"* and *"Are There Any Questions?,"* written and illustrated by Denys Cazet, are two hilarious books about school — the first day of school and a school field trip.

♦ *Metropolitan Cow*, written and illustrated by Tim Egan, tells the humorous story of a young bovine teaching his parents a lesson about snobbery.

♦ *When Bluebell Sang*, written and illustrated by Lisa Campbell Ernst, is another clever cow story. This cow can sing, and does so on the road until she outwits her greedy manager so she and her owner can return home.

♦ *Chrysanthemum*, written and illustrated by Kevin Henkes, tells the tale of Chrysanthemum the mouse-child who loves her name until she starts school. Who can spell such a long moniker? Why, everyone's favorite teacher, of course.

♦ *The Cow Who Wouldn't Come Down*, written and illustrated by Paul Brett Johnson, is about an old lady, her cow, and the fake cow she stitches together to lure her cow out of the sky. It is a silly, fun-filled story with a wordless, comic twist on the final page.

♦ *Sherman the Sheep*, written by Kevin Kiser and illustrated by Rowan Barnes-Murphy, is Bill's favorite picture book. Sherman is the smartest sheep in the valley who leads his flock to the best field in the valley, singing as they go around and . . . back to where they started.

♦ *Tacky the Penguin*, written by Helen Lester and illustrated by Lynn Munsinger, is about an odd sort of bird who comes to the rescue of his conventional companions.

♦ *Sheep in a Jeep*, written by Nancy Shaw and illustrated by Margot Apple, and its rollicking sequels mix rhyme with wit in a series of sheep adventures.

♦ *Don't Fidget a Feather!*, written by Erica Silverman and illustrated by S. D. Schindler, features a contest between Duck and Gander to see who can freeze in place the longest.

I always laugh at the page when a stiff wind blows them into the bushes.

◆ *Glasses, Who Needs 'Em?,* written and illustrated by Lane Smith, makes anyone want to wear spectacles.

◆ *Somebody and the Three Blairs*, written by Marilyn Tolhurst and illustrated by Simone Abel, is the funniest retelling of a familiar fairy tale in our home library.

◆ *Max's Dragon Shirt*, written and illustrated by Rosemary Wells, inspires guffaws when Max figures out that the bunny-person he has been following in the department store isn't his sister Ruby, but a teenager, complete with hot pink lipstick and earrings in her rabbit ears. In *Bunny Money*, Max and Ruby again go on a priceless shopping trip, this time for a present for Grandma.

◆ *Tuesday*, written and illustrated by David Wiesner, is a nearly wordless picture book in which frogs fly around town and in and out of houses.

There are a handful of picture book authors whose every book is filled with wit: Dr. Seuss, William Steig, Peggy Rathmann, Daniel Pinkwater, Bill Peet, and the incomparable team of Jon Scieszka and Lane Smith.

For children who are reading on their own or listening to chapter books, Beverly Cleary's "Ramona" books, Lois Lowry's "Sam" and "Anastasia" series, and Eleanor Estes's "Moffat" books embrace humor as well as warmth. Jennifer and Allison also laughed their way all the way through *The Best Christmas Pageant Ever* and *The Best School Year Ever*, Barbara Robinson's books about the horrible but lovable Herdmans.

Many of the finest children's authors use humor to make their stories even richer. Natalie Babbitt brilliantly sprinkles comic moments in her otherwise serious and compelling novel, *Tuck Everlasting*. Nancy Farmer's books always exhibit wittiness in the midst of a great story. And there is one line in Patricia MacLachlan's *Baby* that cracks me up every time I read it. (Hint: it has to do with the identity of "Wild Eunice.")

Whether for pure reading enjoyment or cheering-up purposes, we will often reach for a book that makes us laugh. Funny, isn't it? 🐛

Books

Babbitt, Natalie, *Tuck Everlasting* (1975)

Brown, Jeff, *Flat Stanley*, illustrated by Tomi Ungerer (1964)

Cazet, Denys, *"Never Spit on Your Shoes"* (1990); *"Are There Any Questions?"* (1992)

Clements, Andrew, *Frindle*, illustrated by Brian Selznick (1996)

Curtis, Christopher Paul, *The Watsons Go to Birmingham — 1963* (1995)

Egan, Tim, *Metropolitan Cow* (1996)

Ernst, Lisa Campbell, *When Bluebell Sang* (1989)

Farmer, Nancy, *Do You Know Me*, illustrated by Shelley Jackson (1993); *The Ear, the Eye and the Arm* (1994); *The Warm Place* (1995); *A Girl Named Disaster* (1996)

Henkes, Kevin, *Chrysanthemum* (1991)

Johnson, Paul Brett, *The Cow Who Wouldn't Come Down* (1993)

Kiser, Kevin, *Sherman the Sheep*, illustrated by Rowan Barnes-Murphy (1994)

Lester, Helen, *Tacky the Penguin*, illustrated by Lynn Munsinger (1988)

MacLachlan, Patricia, *Baby* (1993)

Meddaugh, Susan, *Martha Speaks* (1992); *Martha Calling* (1994); *Martha Blah Blah* (1996)

Peet, Bill, *Hubert's Hair-Raising Adventure* (1959); *Randy's Dandy Lions* (1964); *Chester the Worldly Pig* (1965); *The Wump World* (1970), and others

Pinkwater, Daniel, *The Big Orange Splot* (1977); *Aunt Lulu* (1988); *Author's Day* (1993), and others

Robinson, Barbara, *The Best Christmas Pageant Ever* (1972); *The Best School Year Ever* (1994)

Sachar, Louis, *Wayside School Gets a Little Stranger*, illustrated by Joel Schick (1995)

Shaw, Nancy, *Sheep in a Jeep*, illustrated by Margot Apple (1986)

Silverman, Erica, *Don't Fidget a Feather!*, illustrated by S. D. Schindler (1994)

Smith, Lane, *Glasses, Who Needs 'Em?* (1991)

Tolhurst, Marilyn, *Somebody and the Three Blairs*, illustrated by Simone Abel (1990)

Wells, Rosemary, *Max's Dragon Shirt* (1991); *Bunny Money* (1997)

Wiesner, David, *Tuesday* (1991)

"Persimmon Ships" and Other Things We Say from Books

Molly was looking worried one morning. "Mom," she said, a minute before she had to leave for school, "where's my persimmon ship? I need to turn it in today."

"It's in your backpack," I reassured her. "I signed it last night."

"Whew," she sighed. "Thanks!" And off she flew.

What's this? Had my first grader carved a sailing vessel out of an orange fruit? Or perhaps the tree? And why in the world would she want me to sign it?

Because Molly was, in fact, talking about a *permission slip* for a field trip. In our household, we call one of those little pieces of paper a "persimmon ship," thanks to a line in our favorite picture book about a school field trip, Denys Cazet's hilarious *"Are There Any Questions?"* It's one of the sayings we picked up from children's books and adapted to our family's lexicon. We also quote Tigger when we burp. "Skoos ee," we say, even though our mouths aren't full of haycorns, as his is in A. A. Milne's *The House at Pooh Corner.* Characters have come to live with us, too, most notably the Boggart, an ancient spirit who loves to play tricks, and whom we first met in Susan Cooper's wildly entertaining book called, simply, *The Boggart.* During one active week last fall, he made off with Allison's script for *Dickens' Christmas Carol* and my *School Library Journal*. What's more, he fooled around with the hard drive on my computer. He is always hiding the kids' sweatshirts and socks. "Okay, Boggart!" we holler. "Where are they?" He never replies, but occasionally he returns them in the most unlikely places — or perhaps precisely where they were all along.

My Connecticut friend, Karen, and her family are luckier. They have a benevolent household spirit living with them: Hob, the funny little character from William Mayne's "Hob Stories." Hob's job is to keep trouble away from the family home, and in *The Red Book of Hob Stories*, he even outwits a Boggart (apparently these mischievous spirits are well known in Great Britain). Hob lives in a "cutch" under the stairs, and, as it turns out, so does Karen's dog. "We borrowed cutch as a nicer word than crate," she told me. When this dog, a big galoot, came to live with them four years ago, Karen's husband started saying, "Merciful heavens, it's a dog!" from *Prehistoric Pinkerton* by Steven Kellogg. The expression stuck. Their cat acts like a modern version of Eleanor Estes's Pinky Pye (from the book of the same name) by punching the buttons that make noise on the fax machine when he wants to be let out. Karen's children have been known to refer to underwear as "underfrillies," a term from Jeanne Willis and Tony Ross's clever Professor Xargle earth alien books. If the kids would like help from their parents, they'll sometimes use a William Joyce expression from *The Leaf Men and the Brave Good Bugs*: "Leaf men, we are in need!" And when Karen was a child, her mother borrowed a line from Maurice Sendak's picture book, *Where the Wild Things Are*, when the family set off on vacation: "Let the wild rumpus start!"

Indeed, when I put out the word (at school, in my writers group, over the Internet, in letters) that I was looking for expressions or characters that have become part of a family's culture, there were several repeat books and authors. *Where the Wild Things Are* was one. I heard about a mother who made "wild rumpus tarts" in honor of her overly active preschooler, and if my survey is any indication, about fifty percent of young American children have been called "wild thing" by their parents. My childhood friend Joyce had a "wild things" birthday party for her (appropriately named) son Max when he turned three. Another Sendak book, *Outside Over There*, inspired a neighbor's family members to refer to one another as an "ice baby" when someone deviates from his or her true self. (The goblins left an ice baby when they took the real baby while the older sister was supposed to be looking after her.)

Dr. Seuss was a genius with words, pictures, and concepts. After reading *Green Eggs and Ham*, how many children (and adults) have insisted, "I do not like them, Sam-I-am," when they are absolutely, positively sure they won't like something new? Peggy, in my writers group, remembers the kids in her family hollering "Hop on Pop!" when they pounced on their father. When the family room in my friend Terry's house turns into a disaster area, she quotes the lines from the finicky fish in *The Cat in the Hat* that begin with, "This mess is so big . . . " And when they haven't listened to that little voice trying to warn them of impending disaster, an online bookstore owner from Colorado reports that she and her family say, "I should have listened to the fish." Dr. Seuss — yep, he was worth listening to.

A. A. Milne, according to my unscientific survey, is the other most frequently quoted children's book author. So many families are like ours and have taken the animals of the Hundred Acre Wood into their hearts and homes. Around here we not only say Tigger's "Skoos ee" on a daily basis, but if the sky looks threatening I might declare, "Tut-tut, it looks like rain," as Pooh asked his friend Christopher Robin to do in *Winnie-the-Pooh*. I heard from dozens of parents who said their children exclaim "Bother!" when something goes wrong. A mom at school and her young children recall as they climb their own stairs at night how Winnie-the-Pooh went *"bump, bump, bump* — going up the stairs . . . " Another writer reported that in her family, a less than intelligent person is "a bear of very little brain."

When Jennifer was eleven, she and some of her friends formed a "Pooh Group," each girl taking on the identity and character of one of the animals in the books. Jennifer was little Roo. It wasn't the first Pooh Group known to our family. My mother and her college friends christened the dreary basement dorm rooms they were assigned to one year "Pooh Corner" and adopted the characters as their own. This Pooh Group of classmates continues to meet twice a year more than half a century after they got together during World War II. Mom was, and still is, Rabbit the organizer.

Jennifer and I tease the aforementioned Rabbit when she wears her rather strong floral perfume. "Grandma Hocky's here!" one of us announces if she arrives at our house surrounded by scent. Grandma Hocky is a character in Lane Smith's silly book, *The Happy Hocky Family*, and her perfume smells like "LOTS and LOTS of FLOWERS." My dear mother swears she isn't at all a Grandma Hocky, but Jennifer and I respectfully disagree.

Charlotte, the best friend a pig could ever have, took the sage advice of her author, E. B. White, and kept her spoken and written words simple throughout *Charlotte's Web*. (Rule 17 in William Strunk and E. B. White's book on writing, *The Elements of Style*: "Omit needless words.") Parents and children alike think of Charlotte when they say, "Salutations!" When a young actor does something well at Palo Alto Children's Theatre, another child may exclaim, "Some pig!" (the first words Charlotte wove in her web). What I think is wonderful is that all the other kids understand the reference.

Using familiar sayings from children's books can help little ones learn life's important lessons. We gave a copy of one of our favorite toddler books, Rachel Isadora's *I Touch*, to my niece Lindsey for her first birthday. The line "I do not touch the cup. It's hot." made such an impression on Lindsey that five years later she still calls her parents' coffee cups "hot-hot." I heard from many parents who use the gentle words in Margaret Wise Brown's little book, *Little Fur Family*, "Bless you, fur child, every time you sneeze." At dinner on the

110

day in which our dog, Bosco, ate six months' worth of anti-flea pills while I was having a nail removed from the tire of my car, Bill quoted Alexander's mother from the final pages of Judith Viorst's *Alexander and the Terrible, Horrible, No Good, Very Bad Day*: " . . . some days are like that. Even in Australia." Liz, from my writers group, reports that in her family they say, "I need a visit to the Bunny Planet," when someone is having a tough time of it, referring to Rosemary Wells's charming *Voyage to the Bunny Planet* collection. Chris Van Allsburg's two simple words, "I believe," in *The Polar Express* are an inspiration for all ages.

Liz's family also borrowed a line uttered by the simpleton in Robert Lawson's *Rabbit Hill*: "Readin' rots the mind." Turns out, of course, that the animal-loving and book-loving new folks in the old farmhouse have fine minds, big hearts, and a flourishing garden to boot — all of which children learn from reading *Rabbit Hill*.

Ludwig Bemelmans's *Madeline* is another eminently quotable book. When my girls were younger and Madeline's story was standard bedtime fare, I would stand at the doorway — Miss Clavel-style — and recite, "Good night little girls! Thank the lord you are well! . . . " Several parents told me that they say, "Something is not right," when they are certain it isn't. Naturally, after Allison had an emergency appendectomy we remarked, "On her stomach was a scar." (Or two or three itty-bitty scars, thanks to modern surgical tools.) Because Allison was only in the hospital overnight, her sisters didn't have time to be jealous of all the attention Bill and I were heaping on her. If she'd stayed for two weeks, however, Jennifer and Molly undoubtedly would have cried, "Boohoo, we want to have our appendix out too!"

Children often recall words or expressions from books years later and use them appropriately. When friends of ours checked into a hotel with their daughters, the girls got an Eloise-like gleam in their eyes and said, "Ooooooooooooooooooo, I absolutely love Room Service," a line from *Eloise*, Kay Thompson's picture book about the precocious girl who lives at the Plaza Hotel. Many families use concepts from their favorite children's books on a daily basis. A friend in Oklahoma and her son blow on the red stop lights to make them change to green (Elizabeth Spurr's *Mrs. Minetta's Car Pool*). The daughter of the art teacher at our school quotes Lewis Carroll from *Alice in Wonderland* ("Do cats eat bats? Do bats eat cats?") when she thinks her mother isn't making sense; and a Tennessee teacher exclaims, "Off with your head!" from *Alice* whenever a student tells her "bad news" such as, "I forgot my lunch money." A boy in Molly's class pretends to be Bendemolina, the character in Jan Slepian and Ann Seidler's *The Cat Who Wore a Pot on Her Head*, when he doesn't hear (or wish to hear) what his parents say to him. When my friend Terrie's sons, Jamie and Justin, are thirsty, they sometimes ask for "frobscottle," the giants' drink in Roald Dahl's *The BFG. Genuine* frobscottle, a drink with bubbles that go down instead of up, has the effect of producing explosive "whizzpoppers" down below, according to Roald Dahl (and Jamie and Justin).

Some sayings are more or less transitory — used while the book is fresh in one's mind. Right after my older daughters read Bette Bao Lord's *In the Year of the Boar and Jackie Robinson*, each would recite daily Shirley Temple Wong's version of the Pledge of Allegiance: "I pledge a lesson to the frog . . ." Another time, Jennifer spouted off to anyone who asked about Natalie Babbitt's *Tuck Everlasting* Winnie Foster's imagined "list of don'ts": "Now remember, Winifred — don't bite your fingernails, don't interrupt when someone else is speaking, and don't go down to the jailhouse at midnight to change places with prisoners." She cracked up every time she said it.

I heard from a Canadian librarian who had been reading Lloyd Alexander's "Prydain" books with his children and doing a lot of Gurgi-talk: snacks are "munchings and crunchings," and having to shovel snow out of the driveway causes many "moanings and groanings." The bookstore owner gets her four-year-old into the bath with help from *Dogzilla*: "No more mister mice guy, it's bathtime!" Jennifer's friend Leah called her mother "Momsy" while she was reading Anne Frank's *The Diary of a Young Girl*.

One of the reasons I was so charmed by Andrew Clements's *Frindle* is that the entire plot revolves around what happens when a new word is added to the vernacular. Why *not* call a pen a frindle? Allison does, and so do I. We know what we mean. Too, every time we use the word "frindle" or call a special friend a "kindred spirit" (from L. M. Montgomery's *Anne of Green Gables*) we are reminded — if only for a moment — of a beloved children's book. By integrating the language of children's literature into our daily lives, we're extending favorite books beyond their final pages.

We are saying that books matter by saying what matters to us from books. ❧

Books

Alexander, Lloyd, *The High King* (1968)
Babbitt, Natalie, *Tuck Everlasting* (1975)
Bemelmans, Ludwig, *Madeline* (1939)
Brown, Margaret Wise, *Little Fur Family*, illustrated by Garth Williams (1946)
Carroll, Lewis, *Alice's Adventures in Wonderland* (1865)
Cazet, Denys, *"Are There Any Questions?"* (1992)
Clements, Andrew, *Frindle*, illustrated by Brian Selznick (1996)
Cooper, Susan, *The Boggart* (1993)
Dahl, Roald, *The BFG*, illustrated by Quentin Blake (1982)
Estes, Eleanor, *Pinky Pye* (1958)
Frank, Anne, *The Diary of a Young Girl* (1952)
Isadora, Rachel, *I Touch* (1985)
Joyce, William, *The Leaf Men and the Brave Good Bugs* (1996)
Kellogg, Steven, *Prehistoric Pinkerton* (1985)
Lawson, Robert, *Rabbit Hill* (1944)
Lord, Bette Bao, *In the Year of the Boar and Jackie Robinson*, illustrated by Marc Simont (1984)

Mayne, William, *The Red Book of Hob Stories* (1984)

Milne, A. A., *Winnie-the-Pooh* (1926); *The House at Pooh Corner* (1928), both illustrated by Ernest Shepard

Montgomery, L. M., *Anne of Green Gables* (1908)

Pilkey, Dav, *Dogzilla* (1993)

Sendak, Maurice, *Where the Wild Things Are* (1963); *Outside Over There* (1987)

Seuss, Dr., *The Cat in the Hat* (1957); *Green Eggs and Ham* (1960); *Hop on Pop* (1963)

Slepian, Jan and Ann Seidler, *The Cat Who Wore a Pot on Her Head* (1980)

Smith, Lane, *The Happy Hocky Family* (1993)

Spurr, Elizabeth, *Mrs. Minetta's Car Pool*, illustrated by Blanche Sims (1985)

Strunk, William J. and E. B. White, *The Elements of Style*, Third Edition (1979)

Thompson, Kay, *Eloise* (1955)

Van Allsburg, Chris, *The Polar Express* (1985)

Viorst, Judith, *Alexander and the Terrible, Horrible, No Good, Very Bad Day*, illustrated by Ray Cruz (1972)

Wells, Rosemary, *Voyage to the Bunny Planet* (1992)

White, E. B., *Charlotte's Web*, illustrated by Garth Williams (1952)

Willis, Jeanne, *Relativity, As Explained by Professor Xargle*, illustrated by Tony Ross (1993)

Books About All Kinds of Families

C hildren exposed to a wide variety of books inevitably meet all kinds of families — families like theirs as well as those that may be quite different. I think this is healthy. By showing what life is like for other children, young readers can't help but become more understanding and tolerant of differences. Perhaps they will also see themselves and their own families reflected in a different light. Authors of picture books, middle-grade readers, and young adult literature are constantly documenting and contemplating "the family" and what it means to be a family.

Depictions of the traditional two-parent family abound in books for young children. Marc Brown's fabulously popular Arthur character appears at first glance to be an aardvark, but he's actually a boy with an annoying younger sister, a cute baby sister, a dog, and two loving parents. The family is his anchor, even when he thinks he would rather be at summer camp with his best friend instead of with his mom, dad, and sisters at the beach in *Arthur's Family Vacation* (our favorite of the "Arthur" books). When my girls were preschoolers, they loved to listen to Shirley Hughes's stories about Alfie and Annie Rose, and study the brightly painted pictures of the messy but adorable siblings who live with their nurturing "mum" and dad somewhere in London. For a fresh twist to the idea of moms working outside the home (or to stay-at-home dads), our choice is *The Daddies Boat*, written by Lucia Monfried and illustrated by Michele Chessare. No matter how many times my kids have heard the story, they still take pleasure in turning the page to see the *mommy* on the deck of the *daddies* ferryboat. One book Molly often asks for, Holly Keller's *Harry and Tuck*, features a pair of identical twins who must separate on the first day of kindergarten. Not to worry, though — by day number two, Harry and Tuck know they'll have a good time in school and still have each other afterwards. They can even dress differently for a change.

When Jennifer was able to read on her own, she went through Beverly Cleary's "Ramona" series and Judy Blume's books about Peter and Fudge, beginning with *Tales of a Fourth Grade Nothing*. All these stories are grounded in the lives of relatively happy, secure, two-parent, middle-class families. A parent may lose a job (*Ramona and Her Father*), or move everyone to a different state (*Superfudge*), but life goes on despite sibling rivalry and minor crises, and there's a happy ending besides. Lois Lowry has created in the Krupnik family another appealing, humorous, loving household of not-so-perfect kids and parents in the "Anastasia" and "Sam" books.

Grandparents also figure prominently in books for little ones. Allison's all-time favorite picture book, *Nana's Birthday Party*, written by Amy Hest and illustrated by Amy Schwartz, tells the comforting story of two cousins spending the night at Nana's house before the big party, and how they collaborate on the perfect gift for their grandmother. Eve Bunting's *The Wednesday Surprise*, illustrated by Donald Carrick, features an ingenious granddaughter who teaches her grandma how to read. In Judith Caseley's *Dear Annie*, a grandfather writes cards or letters every week to his granddaughter, and when Annie is old enough, she writes back. These heartwarming stories remind children and their parents that intergenerational love is something special and worth cultivating.

Middle-grade readers are deemed old enough to understand that elderly grandparents may have special needs, and even faults. In *Utterly Yours, Booker Jones* by Betsy Duffy, Booker's ninety-two-year-old grandfather moves in with his family after a stroke. Life won't ever be the same, Booker realizes, but it doesn't have to be as bad as it was in the weeks right after Pop moved in. The grandfather in Alfred Slote's *The Trading Game* had been a major league baseball player, so naturally baseball-loving Andy idolizes him . . . until Grampa shows his unsportsmanlike side. In both books, the main character comes to a better understanding of his grandfather's shortcomings. And in *The Trading Game*, Andy also knows finally how his deceased father felt about being coached by "Ace 459."

I've loved to read about large families ever since I picked up my first "Bobbsey Twins" book in second grade. When I was older I owned classic, beautiful editions of Margaret Sidney's *The Five Little Peppers and How They Grew* and Louisa May Alcott's *Little Women* (I had three brothers, so any girl with three sisters was worthy of envy in my eyes.) My girls, too, are drawn to stories about big families. For years they've gotten a kick out of the delightful picture book about a girl who tries to capture the attention of her parents and eleven sisters and brothers, *The Catspring Somersault Flying One-handed Flip-flop*, written by SuAnn Kiser and illustrated by Peter Catalanotto. Jennifer also read several books in the popular "All-of-a-Kind Family" series by Sydney Taylor about a Jewish family of five girls and one baby boy growing up in New York in the early part of the twentieth century. Hilary McKay's *The Exiles* and its sequel, *The Exiles at Home*, featuring the humorous "adventures" of four quirky, book-loving sisters, are at the top of our list of favorite books.

Jennifer has been known to complain about being the oldest kid, so one day I handed her *Fig Pudding*, a novel by Ralph Fletcher about a family as observed by the oldest of six children. "It's a good book," she reported later. "Funny, but sad, too. One of the kids gets killed on his bike." Oops, I thought, maybe I should have read it first so I could have prepared her for the death. On the other hand, no one in real life is prepared for accidental death either. "But then they all find something to laugh about by the end of the book," she added.

Death of a sibling is the central theme of *Mick Harte Was Here*, a poignant, hard-to-put-down novel by Barbara Park about a twelve-year-old who thought wearing a bicycle helmet made him look like a "dork," and died when his bike hit a rock and skidded into the back of a truck. Told from the perspective of his older sister, it has comic touches as well as a powerful message about bicycle safety. (I appreciate this, because I'm one of those parents who embarrasses her own children by yelling, "You need a bicycle helmet!" if I see someone else's child riding without one.)

Mick Harte works because it is a strong, believable story about a family in crisis. As an author myself, it's what I tried to do in my picture book, *When Molly Was in the Hospital*. I knew I couldn't simply tell children that having a brother or sister who is sick and in the hospital can really make you jealous and angry. I had to show Anna getting mad when her mother couldn't play with her, or worried that her own anger had made Molly sick. (And because it is a picture book, Nina Ollikainen's sensitive illustrations convey the emotions in pictures.) We show Anna's pride in Molly's recovery, and bring the story full circle as the sisters re-establish their relationship on the last page. Fortunately, libraries have dozens of story books that can help families cope with crises. The best of these books, and the ones worth reading by all families, have memorable characters with something to say.

It seems as if there have been a zillion magazine articles and books written for parents on how to deal with a child's jealousy for her newborn sibling. An enormously funny and clever picture book for kids is Kevin Henkes's *Julius, the Baby of the World*. It was a well-timed coincidence that *Julius* was published the year Molly was born. We all benefited from it. Allison, who was three at the time, made up an entirely new story inspired by big-sister Lilly. Molly now adores the book, too, and she's the youngest kid. Amy Schwartz's *Annabelle Swift, Kindergartner* is another of our best-loved books about a young girl's triumph over her bossy, yet well-meaning older sister. (The unnamed big sister in Bernard Waber's *Ira Sleeps Over*, also an all-time favorite of ours, is much less benevolent than Annabelle's sister Lucy.)

Kids who have annoying younger siblings especially like to see this situation featured in novels they read. In Laurence Yep's *Later, Gator*, a boy gives his super-sweet little brother an alligator for his birthday, and the little guy actually likes it. The pet *almost* manages to make the boys friends. Marilyn Sachs's *Thirteen Going on Seven* depicts twins who are entirely different intellectually, emotionally, and physically. Recently, Jennifer pulled the book out of my office shelf to reread for about the tenth time. "I know I should like the dumb, immature twin, because she's a better person," she said. "But I really like the other girl better. She's cool." (At least my daughter is honest!) Katherine Paterson's Newbery Award-winning *Jacob Have I Loved* is another novel about twin sisters — powerful and moving.

When I was growing up in Orange County, California, an immigrant was considered someone who moved south from Los Angeles. That's not at all the case anymore, in my old hometown or where we live now. Kids from families who emigrated from Russia, China, Japan, Sweden, Norway, Great Britain, Japan, South Korea, El Salvador, Israel, The Netherlands, Greece, Vietnam, and Mexico have been in my daughters' classes — in just the last two years! Our favorite immigrant family in middle-grade novels is the Yangs, of Lensey Namioka's *Yang the Youngest and His Terrible Ear* and *Yang the Third and Her Impossible Family*. The two youngest Yangs try so hard to fit in, and are wonderfully likable characters.

An adult friend of mine whose parents were divorced remembers feeling alone and different. "I wish I had been able to find books about families like mine when I was a child," she said. Now, alas, fractured families are not uncommon, but fortunately for the children of divorce — as well as their friends, which includes about every kid in this country — there are hundreds of good books featuring characters whose parents have split up. Paula Danziger's Amber Brown, the feisty and funny star of *Amber Brown is Not a Crayon* (and its many sequels), deals with this and other problems head on, in true Amber Brown fashion. Leigh Botts, a more serious child/character of divorce, understands by the end of Beverly Cleary's Newbery Award winner, *Dear Mr. Henshaw*, that his parents are better off not living together. In Anne Fine's novel *Step by Wicked Step*, five classmates from divided families spend the night in a mysterious mansion sharing their personal stories.

There are even more children's books in which a child living with one parent isn't a central theme, but a sideline matter of fact. *If Anything Ever Goes Wrong at the Zoo*, written by Mary Jane Hendrick and illustrated by Jane Dyer, is a playful, appealing picture book about a girl who lives alone with her mother and invites the zookeepers to send the animals to her house "if anything ever goes wrong at the zoo" (which, of course, it does). The narrator in Vera B. Williams's *A Chair for My Mother* relates the touching story of how she, her mother, and her grandmother saved all their coins in a big jar until they had enough money to buy an enormous comfy chair for their new apartment after a fire destroyed the furniture in their old house.

For middle-grade readers, Susan Patron's offbeat yet charming *Maybe Yes, Maybe No, Maybe Maybe* features a middle sister named PK who tells her little sister, Rabbit, stories "from the laundry hamper," tries to stay friends with her "Gifted" big sister, Megan, and worries that the new apartment Mama found will present just too much change for the family. Amy Hest's *The Private Notebook of Katie Roberts, Age 11* tells of a sympathetic character's adjustment to living in Texas with her mother and new stepfather after her father's death in World War II. Mia, the narrator of Suzanne Freeman's *The Cuckoo's Child*, must move suddenly from Beruit to Tennessee to live with her aunt when her parents are apparently lost at sea. Mia's adjustment to life back in the United States is far from easy. Junebug, the young hero of Alice Mead's novel *Junebug*, is deathly afraid of the gangs in his decrepit housing project as he approaches his tenth birthday, but finds hope in his dreams of sailing and escaping with his mother and sister from the projects. *Yolanda's Genius*, by Carol Fenner, is another sensitive story about an African-American family headed by a single mom, as Yolanda helps the adults around her recognize her younger brother Andrew's unique musical gift. Extended family members play important roles in *The Cuckoo's Child*, *Junebug*, and *Yolanda's Genius*, just as they do in *A Chair for My Mother* and many real-life single-parent families.

Jennifer has read every book in Phyllis Reynolds Naylor's "Alice" series about a girl growing up with her widowed father. Yet the first book, *The Agony of Alice*, which focuses more on the heroine's sense of loss of living without a mother than the later books do, is her least favorite. (She likes *All but Alice* best.) Nevertheless, Alice is an endearing character, and I'm certain that girls in her situation find more to identify with in the first book than my daughter, whose mother is very much still extant.

Families in books for young adult readers are frequently not strong and secure. Sometimes they're downright dysfunctional. Teen and even preteen readers, who only years before craved humorous stories about happy families with sympathetic, loving parents, may now look for books about homeless or abandoned teens. Kids in middle school today know that some parents neglect or even abuse their children. Families fall apart and kids have to deal with the consequences. Reading about characters who conquer such adversity is helpful not only for children who may have similar problems, but can also be instructive to kids whose biggest gripe with their parents is nagging about homework.

Jamie, the main character in Carolyn Coman's short, intense novel, *What Jamie Saw*, witnesses his stepfather throw his little sister across the room. Em Thurkill, the teenage narrator of Norma Fox Mazer's *When She Was Good*, tells the story of her horrific life with an abusive, disturbed older sister who dies, leaving Em to fend for herself. Gilly, of Katherine Paterson's *The Great Gilly Hopkins*, lives in a series of foster homes because her mother is off "finding herself." In Cynthia Voigt's *Homecoming*, the four Tillerman children, led by thirteen-year-old Dicey, avoid being placed in foster care while they search for their grandmother after their mentally ill mother abandons them in a shopping center parking lot. Yet even though the characters in these books are dealt lousy familial hands, they still come out winners at the end of the game. They find love and even a measure of safety and security by changing, or accepting, or searching until they find a more positive and hopeful family circumstance.

Many of the best works of contemporary children's literature show families triumphing in the midst of crises. In Patricia MacLachlan's *Baby*, Larkin's family is finally able to deal with the death of her baby brother. The Watsons in Christopher Paul Curtis's *The Watsons Go to Birmingham — 1963* pull themselves together after witnessing a racial bombing. The Logan family in Mildred B. Taylor's Newbery Award-winning *Roll of Thunder, Hear My Cry* overcome, in small ways, the cruelly racist, violent society of the rural South in the 1930s. In the final pages of another winner of the Newbery Medal, Virginia Hamilton's *M.C. Higgins, the Great*, M.C., the indomitable hero, gets his family and friends to help him build a wall he hopes will stop mining debris from sliding down the mountain onto their home. Survival comes from conquering, not running away from their fate.

My children are not alone in their fascination for books about families. They want to know: What's it like in other families? How is everyone treated? Who tells the jokes? How would it be to grow up with just a mom or only a dad? How do other kids feel about their place in the birth order? How about bratty or bossy siblings? What's an extended family, anyway? How do fictional families handle hard times? Can we learn anything from the families we only meet in books?

The answer to the last question, whether children are aware of it or not, is most certainly yes. We can learn from fictional families. We are inspired and entertained by their stories, and we gain new insights as we read about their lives — their struggles and their victories — while experiencing our own. 🍎

Books

Alcott, Louisa May, *Little Women* (1867)

Blume, Judy, *Tales of a Fourth Grade Nothing* (1972); *Superfudge* (1980)

Brown, Marc, *Arthur's Family Vacation* (1993)

Bunting, Eve, *The Wednesday Surprise*, illustrated by Donald Carrick (1989)

Caseley, Judith, *Dear Annie* (1991)

Cleary, Beverly, *Ramona and Her Father*, illustrated by Alan Tiegreen (1977); *Dear Mr. Henshaw*, illustrated by Paul O. Zelinsky (1983)

Coman, Carolyn, *What Jamie Saw* (1995)

Curtis, Christopher Paul, *The Watsons Go to Birmingham — 1963* (1995)

Danziger, Paula, *Amber Brown is Not a Crayon*, illustrated by Tony Ross (1994)

Duffy, Betsy, *Utterly Yours, Booker Jones* (1995)

Duncan, Debbie, *When Molly Was in the Hospital: A Book for Brothers and Sisters of Hospitalized Children*, illustrated by Nina Ollikainen, MD (1994)

Fenner, Carol, *Yolanda's Genius* (1995)

Fine, Anne, *Step by Wicked Step* (1996)

Fletcher, Ralph, *Fig Pudding* (1995)

Freeman, Suzanne, *The Cuckoo's Child* (1996)

Hamilton, Virginia, *M. C. Higgins, the Great* (1974)

Hendrick, Mary Jean, *If Anything Ever Goes Wrong at the Zoo*, illustrated by Jane Dyer (1993)

Henkes, Kevin, *Julius, the Baby of the World* (1990)

Hest, Amy, *Nana's Birthday Party*, illustrated by Amy Schwartz (1993)

Hest, Amy, *The Private Notebook of Katie Roberts, Age 11*, illustrated by Sonja Lamut (1995)

Hughes, Shirley, *Alfie Gets in First* (1981); *Alfie Gives a Hand* (1983); *The Big Alfie and Annie Rose Storybook* (1988); *Rhymes for Annie Rose* (1995)

Keller, Holly, *Harry and Tuck* (1993)

Kiser, SuAnn, *The Catspring Somersault Flying One-handed Flip-flop*, illustrated by Peter Catalanotto (1993)

Lowry, Lois, "Anastasia" series; "Sam" series, illustrated by Diane deGroat

MacLachlan, Patricia, *Baby* (1993)

Mazer, Norma Fox, *When She Was Good* (1997)

McKay, Hilary, *The Exiles* (1992); *The Exiles at Home* (1993)

Mead, Alice, *Junebug* (1995)

Monfried, Lucia, *The Daddies Boat*, illustrated by Michele Chessare (1990)

Namioka, Lensey, *Yang the Youngest and His Terrible Ear* (1992); *Yang the Third and Her Impossible Family*, both illustrated by Kees de Kiefte (1995)

Naylor, Phyllis Reynolds, *The Agony of Alice* (1985); *All but Alice* (1992)

Park, Barbara, *Mick Harte Was Here* (1995)

Paterson, Katherine, *The Great Gilly Hopkins* (1978); *Jacob Have I Loved* (1980)

Patron, Susan, *Maybe Yes, Maybe No, Maybe Maybe*, illustrated by Dorothy Donahue (1993)

Sachs, Marilyn, *Thirteen Going on Seven* (1993)

Schwartz, Amy, *Annabelle Swift, Kindergartner* (1988)

Sidney, Margaret, *The Five Little Peppers and How they Grew* (1881)

Slote, Alfred, *The Trading Game* (1990)

Taylor, Mildred B., *Roll of Thunder, Hear My Cry* (1976)

Taylor, Sydney, *All-of-a-Kind-Family* (1951)

Voigt, Cynthia, *Homecoming* (1981)

Waber, Bernard, *Ira Sleeps Over* (1972)

Williams, Vera B., *A Chair for My Mother* (1982)

Yep, Laurence, *Later, Gator* (1995)

Historical Fiction

friend of mine confessed recently, "If I had read historical fiction as a child, I might have actually understood history." History can be more than memorizing the names of presidents and dates of wars. It's also about ordinary people doing extraordinary — or even ordinary — things, and learning something in the process. Children can actually play a part in history. As Newbery Award-winning author Karen Cushman said in an interview on National Public Radio, historical fiction is important because it "helps us find our place in the continuum of history." What happened in the past affects what is happening today; what is happening today may indeed affect the future. Knowing that makes us more responsible citizens.

Our family has been enjoying historical fiction for years. One of Allison's favorite picture books is a work of historical fiction. *Baseball Saved Us*, by Ken Mochizuki and illustrated by Dom Lee, is a moving account of life in a Japanese-American internment camp during World War II. The story struck a chord with my daughter when she was in kindergarten. Allen Say's incredible *Grandfather's Journey*, winner of the Caldecott Medal, is another historical fiction picture book about Japanese Americans and the meaning of home that we keep on our favorite books shelf. I have been fascinated by the Gold Rush era of California's history since I first studied it in fourth grade, so Sonia Levitin's realistic yet warmhearted tale of a girl and her family's trip to California by stagecoach, *Nine for California*, is among my top historical fiction picture books. My kids like it, too.

Karen Cushman turned her considerable writing talents to the same period in her novel *The Ballad of Lucy Whipple*. Twelve-year-old California Morning Whipple (who changes her name to Lucy) arrives in the California mining town of Lucky Diggins in the summer of 1849 with her widowed mother, brother, and two younger sisters. Though she helps her mother run the boarding house for miners, Lucy longs to return to the civilized life of her Massachusetts homeland, especially the library (a girl after my own heart). In the end, she discovers the home she never imagined she would find in the hills of her adopted state, as a pioneer librarian, no less.

In her books Karen Cushman never glosses over the hardships characters face; her tenacious, tough-minded heroines tackle adversity in nearly every chapter. Young readers appreciate this, as do critics. *Catherine, Called Birdy*, Cushman's first book, a fictionalized journal kept by an opinionated thirteen-year-old daughter of a country knight in the year 1290, won a Newbery Honor. Her next book, *The Midwife's Apprentice*, won the Newbery Medal. *The Midwife's Apprentice* is also set in medieval England, but in this story the main character is homeless. Like California/Lucy, her name also changes — from Brat, Dung Beetle or Beetle — to Alyce. The self-named Alyce becomes the midwife's apprentice, who learns to take risks as she "fills her belly" and finds her own place in the world. This is an unpretentious, yet powerful tale.

Katherine Paterson's *Lyddie* tells the story of a Vermont farm girl's experiences in a gritty mill factory in Lowell, Massachusetts in the 1840s. Lyddie returns as a teacher in *Jip: His Story*, Paterson's novel that aims its critical eye not on working conditions, but on slavery and poor farms. Both *Lyddie* and *Jip* are thought-provoking books about memorable characters who deal with painful, difficult issues. This was a period in American history that indeed should not be forgotten.

Also not to be forgotten is our nation's bloodiest conflict, the Civil War. When I started kindergarten in 1958, it was still acceptable playground chatter to ask which side your family fought on in that war. (Like many Californians, I was the product of a mixed marriage — my father's family was from the South; my mother's, the North.) David, my oldest brother, was fascinated by the Civil War. Often I would listen with him to the records he collected; I loved the songs, but the gory black-and-white battle photographs on the albums frightened me. David would have loved Paul Fleischman's intense and instructive historical novel about the characters who took part in the first major battle of the Civil War, *Bull Run*. Told from the points of view of sixteen male and female, Northern and Southern participants, it is a heartbreaking and emotional book. These people are scared, determined, confused, brave, stupid, and proud. Now I know why the music to come from the war was so spectacular — at least at the beginning of the conflict, musicians played for the soldiers as they marched. What I didn't know until I read *Bull Run* was that certain wealthy Washington citizens and congressmen hired coaches to take them to a picnic spot above the battlefield, " . . . to watch the thrashing of the Rebs." Alas, they were in for a rude awakening as the South won that battle. The war was on.

The immigrant experience is expertly and meaningfully portrayed by the Chinese-American writer Laurence Yep in his two Newbery Honor books, *Dragonwings* and *Dragon's Gate*. *Dragonwings* takes place in San Francisco in the early 1900s, and *Dragon's Gate* is set in the Sierra Nevada in 1867 during the construction of the transcontinental railroad. Both books are about family and cultural understanding, as well as about the Chinese in America.

Kit, the main character in Elizabeth George Speare's stunning Newbery Award winner, *The Witch of Blackbird Pond*, was an immigrant to New England nearly one hundred years before the Declaration of Independence. This novel makes Puritan witch hunts seem real even to modern readers. Jennifer and her friends considered this one of the best books they read in fifth grade. They *were* Kit; they felt deeply for her. And through her they realized that witch hunts didn't end with the Salem Witch Trials of 1692 (when, by the way, my husband's ancestor, John Proctor, was hanged). *The Witch of Blackbird Pond* prompted discussions about the McCarthy era, gay bashing, and rumors getting out of control even at an elementary school.

The American prairie is the setting for three poignant historical novels I like a lot — *Sarah, Plain and Tall* by Patricia MacLachlan (winner of the Newbery Medal); *Prairie Songs* by Pam Conrad; and *Black-Eyed Susan* by Jennifer Armstrong. In *Sarah*, a family hopes a mail-order bride from the coast of Maine will stay with them on the prairie, " . . . where there were fields and grass and sky and not much else." MacLachlan told a group at a writers conference that she carries a bag of prairie dirt with her at all times. In her evocative prose, a reader can feel the vastness of the American frontier on every page. In *Prairie Songs* and *Black-Eyed Susan*, children who love the prairie must deal with adults who are depressed by the enormity and loneliness of it all. *Black-Eyed Susan* reminds me of *Sarah, Plain and Tall*. The characterizations of Susie, her family, and the family that passes through for the night are exquisite.

The first historical fiction series Jennifer read was from "American Girl" — not great literature, but the books are useful in showing how ordinary girls lived in the past. Jennifer's favorite historical fiction series, though, is Joan Lowery Nixon's "The Orphan Train Adventures," which tell the stories of one or more of the six Kelly children sent from New York to their new homes in St. Joseph, Missouri in 1860. Originally a quartet of books, beginning with *A Family Apart*, the "Orphan Train" series has grown to seven books (and counting), delighting my daughter and thousands of other middle-grade fans of these books.

Molly, at six, became enthralled with the "Little House" books by (and about) Laura Ingalls Wilder after Molly's first-grade teacher began reading the series to her class. (Molly's older sisters were turned off by the descriptions of killing of animals — even for food — in the "Little House" books, so they didn't read more than one. To each her own.) I will encourage Molly to reread the books to herself in a couple of years. There is a new historical fiction series catching on with older readers called "Dear America," where each book is a fictionalized diary of a young girl in a different historical period.

Joan W. Blos won the Newbery Medal for a historical novel in journal form, *A Gathering of Days: A New England Girl's Journal, 1830-32*. I find the book fascinating. Historically significant issues such as how — or even if — to help a runaway slave are important for thirteen-year-old Catherine to write about, yet so is the weather. Another Blos book I couldn't put down is *Brooklyn Doesn't Rhyme*, a charming series of vignettes about a Jewish immigrant family at the turn of the century.

All of these books make the past come alive for young readers, and that's a good thing. Reading historical fiction helps kids understand that the world did not begin the day they were born, that there were those who came before them — people (children, even!) who had feelings, hopes, dreams, fears, and unique problems. Historical fiction takes children beyond their present, everyday lives. And that is also a good thing. 🐾

Books

Armstrong, Jennifer, *Black-Eyed Susan* (1995)
Blos, Joan W., *A Gathering of Days: A New England Girl's Journal, 1930-32* (1979); *Brooklyn Doesn't Rhyme* (1994)

Conrad, Pam, *Prairie Songs* (1985)

Cushman, Karen, *Catherine, Called Birdy* (1994); *The Midwife's Apprentice* (1995); *The Ballad of Lucy Whipple* (1996)

Fleischman, Paul, *Bull Run*, woodcuts by David Frampton (1993)

Levitin, Sonia, *Nine for California*, illustrated by Cat Bowman Smith (1996)

MacLachlan, Patricia, *Sarah, Plain and Tall* (1985)

Mochizuki, Ken, *Baseball Saved Us*, illustrated by Dom Lee (1993)

Nixon, Joan Lowery, "The Orphan Train Adventures," including *A Family Apart* (1987)

Paterson, Katherine, *Lyddie* (1991); *Jip: His Story* (1996)

Say, Allen, *Grandfather's Journey* (1993)

Speare, Elizabeth George, *The Witch of Blackbird Pond* (1958)

Wilder, Laura Ingalls, "Little House" series, illustrated by Garth Williams (1932-1943)

Yep, Laurence, *Dragonwings* (1975); *Dragon's Gate* (1993)

Also . . .

Various Authors, "Dear America" series
Various Authors, "American Girl" series

Nonfiction

I admit it: I have a fiction bias. When I think about my absolute favorite children's books, every one is fiction. Nonfiction makes me think of the books we *need* — for Allison's dreaded missions report or Jennifer's boring Roman drama poster, for instance — not books we necessarily *want* to have for our home library. Okay, having said that, I also realize the following:

A) Not all families are like mine. Obviously, I have all girls, and nonfiction is more popular with boys. Some boys I meet at the checkout desk at the school library *only* read nonfiction, and read a lot of it, too — books about animals, drawing, dinosaurs, people, science, cars, sports, whatever. Lee J. Ames drawing books and Dorothy Hinshaw Patent animal books are extremely popular with middle-grade boys and girls.

B) There are several nonfiction books we know and love just as much as our fiction, beginning with some beautifully illustrated picture books.

Gloria Houston's *My Great-Aunt Arizona*, illustrated by Susan Condie Lamb, is a touching biography of an Appalachian girl who grew up to be a beloved teacher. *Humphrey: The Lost Whale*, written by Wendy Tokuda and

Richard Hall, and illustrated by Hanako Wakiyama, is another well-thumbed picture book on our shelf, telling the exciting story of the humpback whale who took a wrong turn into San Francisco Bay when Jennifer was a baby. David Schwartz and Stephen Kellogg's *How Much is a Million?* is our favorite math concept book. Similarly, Joanna Cole and Bruce Degen's "Magic School Bus" series conveys scientific concepts in fascinating and funny ways. Allison collected the entire set — and read it, too. The Smithsonian Institution publishes a wonderful series of storybooks about wildlife, usually featuring baby animals that are appealing to young children. Two of the best are *Dolphin's First Day*, written by Kathleen Weidner Zoehfeld and illustrated by Steven James Petruccio, and *The Ice's Edge: The Story of a Harp Seal Pup*, written by Karen Romano Young and illustrated by Brian Shaw.

Nonfiction is most useful when kids want to know more about something they're interested in. Because my girls are actors at heart, they have read and studied Jill Krementz's excellent photo essay, *A Very Young Actress*, one in a series of books about children who are incredibly serious about their hobbies. *Onstage/Backstage*, another household favorite, is a photo essay by Caryn Huberman and JoAnne Stewart Wetzel about our very own Palo Alto Children's Theatre, the oldest theater company in the United States where all the actors are children. After Jennifer played a schoolgirl in the Palo Alto Children's Theatre play *Hans Christian Andersen*, we checked out Beth Wagner Brust's *The Amazing Paper Cuttings of Hans Christian Andersen*, an informative book about another side of the genius of the great storyteller. I'm a lifetime fan of libraries, so I found Julie Cummins and Roxie Munro's picture book, *The Inside-Outside Book of Libraries*, particularly illuminating.

For pure facts, my kids recommend *The Guinness Book of World Records*. We buy a new edition every year, and because the girls pick it up so frequently, every week I find it in a different child's room. A new book, Karen Romano Young's *Guinness Record Breakers*, tells fascinating stories about the people who set the records. We love it. Allison studies *The World Almanac for Kids* for, as she says, "Interesting facts about places all over the world." She also sat down and read through a gorgeous coffee table book about kids around the world, Barnabas and Anabel Kindersley's *Children Just Like Me*, as soon as I brought it home.

When I was a child, there were precious few biographies of women and their accomplishments. I am pleased to note that's not the case anymore. I have some favorites, and I'm always on the lookout for more. *Bloomers!,* written by Rhoda Blumberg and illustrated by Mary Morgan, is an engaging picture book about pioneers in the American women's rights movement and the clothes they wore. Both Jennifer and Allison followed that book with Jean Fritz's immensely readable biography of the great Elizabeth Cady Stanton, *You Want Women to Vote, Lizzie Stanton?* Don Brown's *Ruth Law Thrills a Nation* is an intriguing picture book about a female aviation pioneer. And in Kathleen Krull's *Wilma Unlimited: How Wilma Rudolph Became the World's Fastest Woman*, strikingly illustrated by Caldecott Medalist David Diaz, children learn of the extraordinary courage and determination of a three-time Olympic gold medal winner who had once been crippled with polio.

I left another book about a polio survivor, Peg Kehret's *Small Steps: The Year I Got Polio*, with Jennifer one summer night after read-aloud time. "I've heard great things about this book, Jen," I said. "I'd like to know what you think."

Next morning she emerged bleary-eyed from her bedroom even later than usual. "Did you read it?" I asked as she plopped onto the couch.

"Yes, and I finished it, too. Ohmigosh, it's a *great* book," she raved. "After you left I read the table of contents and thought to myself, this is going to be really depressing."

"So?"

"So I reread *A Fate Totally Worse than Death* and *Girl Goddess #9*, then I made myself start *Small Steps*.

I didn't stop until I finished it at 3:10 in the morning. It's as good as any novel." Coming from a fiction fanatic, that's quite an endorsement.

Some kids will latch onto a topic and not let go until they've read everything on the subject. One perennial favorite with young readers is the *Titanic*. Although there have been many novels written about the infamous 1912 disaster (most recently, Barbara Williams's *Titanic Crossing*), the best book for children is the true story by the scientist who led the expedition to find the ship, Robert Ballard's *Exploring the Titanic*. I was a Helen Keller and Abraham Lincoln girl myself. No biography of the amazing Helen Keller stands above the rest, but Russell Freedman's *Lincoln: A Photobiography* is of such high literary quality that it was awarded the Newbery Medal.

Where would we be without those wild and crazy, terrific-looking, information-packed Klutz books about all the things kids really want to know how to do? The creative folks at Klutz Press have a way of figuring out exactly what kids want — to learn how to make a French braid (*Braids and Bows*), friendship bracelet (*Friendship Bracelets*), or Cat's Cradle (*Cat's Cradle: A Book of String Figures*); entertain themselves on car trips (*Kids Travel: A Backseat Survival Kit*) or create clay jewelry (*The Incredible Clay Book*); cook (*Magic Spoon Cookbook*) or blend (*Smoothies*) something yummy; paint a face (*Face Painting*) or fingernail (*Nail Art*); sing a silly song (*Kids Songs*); or visit a kids science museum in a book (*Explorabook*). These are just some of the clever, easy-to-follow Klutz activity books that have been big hits with my kids and their friends over the years.

The best nonfiction books for children — whether they are about science, nature, history, people, places, or things — satisfy a child's innate curiosity about the world. They grab the reader's attention. There are great books about religion (*Bat Mitzvah*), sex (*It's Perfectly Normal*), and money (*The Buck Book*). I hope for future California fourth graders (and their parents) that there will someday be a few good (I'd settle for one or two) books about California missions. For lo and behold, we discovered a book for Jennifer's Roman drama poster that was both fun and fact-filled: Andrew Langley and Philip de Souza's *The Roman News*. Jennifer borrowed a copy from her friend Anna while she was working on the project, and later I bought one for us . . . even though we didn't need it any more. ❦

Books

Ames, Lee J., *Draw 50 Animals* (1974); *Draw 50 Cats* (1986); *Draw 50 Cars, Trucks, and Motorcycles* (1986)

Ballard, Robert, *Exploring the Titanic* (1988)

Block, Francesca Lia, *Girl Goddess #9: Nine Stories* (1996)

Blumberg, Rhoda, *Bloomers!*, illustrated by Mary Morgan (1993)

Brown, Don, *Ruth Law Thrills a Nation* (1993)

Brust, Beth Wagner, *The Amazing Paper Cuttings of Hans Christian Andersen* (1994)

Cassidy, John and The Exploratorium, *Explorabook: A Kids' Science Museum in a Book* (1991)

Cassidy, Nancy, *Kids Songs*, illustrated by Jim M'Guinness (1986)

Cole, Joanna, *The Magic School Bus at the Waterworks*, illustrated by Bruce Degen (1986), and other books in the "Magic School Bus" series

Cummins, Julie, *The Inside-Outside Book of Libraries*, illustrated by Roxie Munro (1996)

Freedman, Russell, *Lincoln: A Photobiography* (1987)

Fritz, Jean, *You Want Women to Vote, Lizzie Stanton?*, illustrated by Anne DiSalvo-Ryan (1995)

Goldin, Barbara Diamond, *Bat Mitzvah: A Jewish Girl's Coming of Age*, illustrated by Erika Weihs (1995)

Gooding, Suzanne, *Magic Spoon Cookbook* (1997)

The Guinness Book of World Records (1997)

Haab, Sherri, *Nail Art* (1997)

Haab, Sherri and Laura Torres, *The Incredible Clay Book* (1994)

Harris, Robie, *It's Perfectly Normal: Growing Up, Sex, and Sexual Health*, illustrated by Michael Emberley (1994)

Houston, Gloria, *My Great-Aunt Arizona*, illustrated by Susan Condie Lamb (1992)

Huberman, Caryn and JoAnne Stewart Wetzel, *Onstage/Backstage* (1987)

Johnson, Anne Akers, *Cat's Cradle: A Book of String Figures* (1993); *The Buck Book* (1993); *Smoothies* (1997)

Johnson, Anne Akers and Robin Stoneking, *Braids and Bows* (1992)

Kehret, Peg, *Small Steps: The Year I Got Polio* (1996)

Kindersley, Barnabas and Anabel, *Children Just Like Me* (1995)

Klutz Press Editors, *Face Painting* (1990); *Kids Travel: A Backseat Survival Kit* (1994)

Krementz, Jill, *A Very Young Actress* (1991)

Krull, Kathleen, *Wilma Unlimited: How Wilma Rudolph Became the World's Fastest Woman*, illustrated by David Diaz (1996)

Langley, Andrew and Philip de Souza, *The Roman News* (1996)

Patent, Dorothy Hinshaw, *Gray Wolf, Red Wolf*, photographs by William Munoz (1990); *Killer Whales*, photographs by John K. B. Ford (1993); *Horses*, photographs by William Munoz (1994)

Schwartz, David, *How Much is a Million?*, illustrated by Steven Kellogg (1985)

Tokuda, Wendy and Richard Hall, *Humphrey the Lost Whale: A True Story*, illustrated by Hanako Wakiyama (1986)

Torres, Laura, *Friendship Bracelets* (1996)

Williams, Barbara, *Titanic Crossing* (1995)

The World Almanac for Kids (1997)

Young, Karen Romano, *Guinness Record Breakers* (1997)

Young, Karen Romano, *The Ice's Edge: The Story of a Harp Seal Pup*, illustrated by Brian Shaw (1996)

Zoehfeld, Kathleen Weidner, *Dolphin's First Day: The Story of a Bottlenose Dolphin*, illustrated by Steven James Petruccio (1994)

Young Adult (Teen) Books

This teenage stuff is new territory for me as a parent. Jennifer isn't yet thirteen. She is an excellent sixth-grade student at a large middle school in Palo Alto. Her gem-of-a-teacher is a family friend. She herself has many friends and (usually) gets along well with her younger sisters. She talks a lot on the phone. She's been in more than a dozen plays and even has had some paid acting jobs. She's a happy kid. I'm not sure I'm ready for her to be going on group dates, but so far I've acquiesced. (The boy she is "going out with" gave her a dozen roses for Valentine's Day.) But here's the part that scares the wits out of me: She knows kids at school who drink alcohol and use drugs. Some of them ride on the bus with her. I repeat, she is in the sixth grade.

Jennifer shared this disturbing news with me the night after she finished reading a young adult novel I had received as a freebie at an award dinner — Francesca Lia Block's *Girl Goddess #9: Nine Stories*. Jennifer read it in two evenings. She hadn't been that engrossed in a book since she picked up *The Face on the Milk Carton*, the book by Caroline B. Cooney about a girl who discovers that she'd been kidnapped years earlier. For a long time I've asked Jennifer to preview books for me, but perhaps in this case I should have been the one to read it first. The day after Jennifer finished *Girl Goddess*, while she was safely (ha ha) at school, I read some of the reviews. *School Library Journal* mentioned " . . . harsh slang, casual sex, drugs, and drinking."[1] (It also put the book on its best books of the year list — for grades nine and up.) The review in *The Horn Book Magazine* cautioned that "Block continues to push at the limitations of 'appropriate' content in young adult books."[2] Whoops! And I encouraged my twelve-year-old to read it? Looks like the "book expert" made a boo-boo. And yet . . . Block is an extraordinarily gifted writer, and I think Jennifer's reading about a teen dying from an overdose of heroin helped her feel more comfortable about talking with me about drugs — drugs in her school, and drugs in general. It was a conversation we needed to have.

The way I look at it, my preteen is being exposed to painful social issues at school. I can't shelter her from the harsh realities of contemporary life, but I can try to give her tools to help her cope with the challenges of the next several years. Part of that includes introducing her to well-written books that are honest depictions of adolescent culture, stories about teens who are also struggling with the social and psychological hurdles of modern adolescence. Teens *should* be reading young adult novels, instead of not reading at all or heading straight to the classics or the latest adult bestseller. Adolescence, when issues such as identity and responsibility are paramount, is a different time of life than any other. It demands its own literature and widespread readership. Even kids who are not strong readers — perhaps *especially* those who are not strong readers — need to know about books written for and about them. (The American Library Association recognizes this. Every year it publishes a list, available at public libraries and on the ALA Web site, of the best books for the "reluctant reader.")

---

[1] Schene, Carol, Review of *Girl Goddess #9: Nine Stories* in *School Library Journal*, 42:9 (September 1996).

[2] Mercier, Cathryn M., Review of *Girl Goddess #9: Nine Stories* in *The Horn Book Magazine*, 72:6 (November/December 1996).

S. E. Hinton's landmark book, *The Outsiders*, is considered by many to be the first realistic young adult novel. Robert Lipsyte's *The Contender* and Robert Cormier's *The Chocolate War* also describe real-life teenage problems and issues. These books are still being read by teens more than twenty or thirty years after they were first published. Other authors who consistently write thoughtful, page-turning young adult novels include: Joan Aiken, Avi, Judy Blume, Bruce Brooks, Lois Duncan, Nancy Farmer, Anne Fine, Nancy Garden, Virginia Hamilton, Karen Hesse, Will Hobbs, M. E. Kerr, Kathryn Lasky, Chris Lynch, Walter Dean Myers, Gary Paulsen, Richard Peck, Philip Pullman, Colby Rodowsky, Cynthia Voigt, Jill Paton Walsh, and Chris Crutcher. I read Crutcher's *Staying Fat for Sarah Byrnes* and was blown away by its power and honesty. I couldn't help wishing there had been books like this when I was in high school. His other contemporary books about sports and life, including *Athletic Shorts, Stotan!, Running Loose,* and *Ironman* have won him legions of fans among teenage boys *and* girls.

Young teens who want to read about adolescent romance can find more than a formulaic "Sweet Valley High" offering. Ellen Wittlinger's *Lombardo's Law* is a charming story with believable, well-drawn characters. *Absolutely Normal Chaos* by Sharon Creech has young love as one of its themes. Rachel Vail writes convincingly of teen pressures to conform in *Ever After, Do-Over, Wonder,* and *Daring to be Abigail.* Jennifer has reread several times Lucy Frank's *I Am an Artichoke,* a book about a fifteen-year-old who starts off as a mother's helper and ends up being more of a mother to her twelve-year-old charge, a girl who has anorexia and a messed-up family life. Girls will find much to appreciate and learn from reading any of these books.

Historical fiction remains strong for the young adult reader. Two authors I like are Kathryn Lasky (*The Bone Wars, Beyond the Burning Time*) and Jennifer Armstrong (*Steal Away, The Dreams of Mairhe Mehan: A Novel of the*

Civil War). Eve Bunting's *Spying on Miss Müller* paints an accurate picture of school girl life in Northern Ireland during World War II. Trudy Krisher's exceptional book, *Spite Fences*, is set in the South at the beginning of the Civil Rights era against a backdrop of prejudice and injustice.

I read Virginia Euwer Wolff's unique and moving novel, *Make Lemonade*, during a writers conference at which the book was being honored. Wolff is a writer who knows her stuff — the way her inner city adolescent characters talk, their worries and goals (both immediate and long-term), and how even the most impoverished teenage mother can "make lemonade" out of the "lemons" in her life if she has grit, determination, and a darn good friend and baby sitter. I was so impressed with the book that I gave it to my sixteen-year-old niece, who loves poetry and a good story (*Make Lemonade* is written entirely in verse). It was Julia's favorite book of the year.

Issues of personal identity for many teens involve questions of sexual identity. Already, Jennifer tells me, girls who exchange hugs at her school are open to accusations of being lesbians. I wish they would read *Deliver Us from Evie* or *Annie on My Mind*, two sensitive love stories involving yes, teenage girls. I hope girls who would recognize themselves in these books manage to find them. *Damned Strong Love: The Story of Willi G. and Stefan K.* is the story of a teenage boy and his love affair with a German soldier during World War II. There are also two incredible novels for the young adult reader dealing with fathers of teens dying of AIDS: *Earthshine* and *The Eagle Kite*.

Not all serious young adult books have to be *serious*. Paul Fleischman won a Newbery Medal for his poetry (*Joyful Noise: Poems for Two Voices*), but his parody of teenage horror novels, *A Fate Totally Worse than Death*, is the book that earned him highest honors in my house. "This is the best book!" Jennifer went on after the first time she read it the summer before sixth grade. "It's hilarious." She gets the jokes, even without ever having read a "Fear Street" saga. Jennifer probably read it a dozen times in six months. We sent a copy to her Pennsylvania friend, Leah, who quickly e-mailed her thanks for the birthday present and an echo of Jennifer's praise. "Great book!" she wrote. (I think Fleischman's short sentences in *A Fate Totally Worse than Death* encourage the same in his readers.)

So there is levity in books for teens, but the standard young adult fare deals with serious, difficult issues of the imperfect world teenagers are inheriting — drug and alcohol abuse, dysfunctional families, poverty, crime, depression, homophobia, homosexuality, suicide, violence, incest, injustice, teenage pregnancy, death, homelessness, abortion, AIDS, sex and sexual abuse, and racism. Not easy themes, but manageable, at least some of the time. Teenagers need to read to find out.

Jennifer cringed slightly when I told her I planned to read *Girl Goddess*. "There are a lot of swear words in that book, Mom," she warned me. Then she added with a grin, "That's one of the things I like about it." I would like to know why this book is so appealing to her and the critics, but I hasten to add that I don't feel I need to read everything my daughters read during their teen years. They deserve some privacy. Besides, our literary tastes aren't as much in sync as they used to be. (The same thing happened with music. So who's surprised?) Both Jennifer and I did, though, fall under the spell of Paul Fleischman's *Seedfolks*, a touching novel about the beauty and power of an inner city garden. She read it in one sitting, and a week later I found her sprawled over the easy chair in her room, "reading the best parts again," as she put it.

I'll continue to visit the library and bookstore for material to bring home for Jennifer to choose from, as well as point out interesting articles in newspapers and magazines. Now that I know she likes Francesca Lia Block, I'll look for the books in the *Weetzie Bat* series. She enjoyed *Daring to be Abigail*, so I'll pick up Rachel Vail's earlier books. If she takes a liking to Cynthia Voigt's *Homecoming*, I'll get the sequel, *Dicey's*

Song. And if Jennifer just wants to go to bed with her *Seventeen* magazine, that's okay too. She's developing her own appreciation of literature in its many forms, and I have to trust that after twelve years of my coaching she'll be intelligent about her choices (well, most of the time).

It's somewhat like the evening meal at our house — Bill and I offer a variety of interesting, tasty and nutritious foods, and the girls are welcome to eat what's put in front of them, or not. It's up to them. They may request certain items be added to the menu, of course. And as they get older and on more friendly terms with the kitchen, they may supplement or replace what's put on the table with something they cook for themselves.

My children are going to be on their own someday. From what my friends who have older kids tell me, it will happen faster than I realize. Their father and I are determined to do all we can to help them learn to make responsible choices in life — about careers, friends, health, recreation, books. Being a parent isn't easy, but I can't imagine anything in the world more important. 🍂

Books

Aiken, Joan, *The Shadow Guests* (1980); *Is Underground* (1993); *Cold Shoulder Road* (1996); *The Cockatrice Boys* (1996), and others

Armstrong, Jennifer, *Steal Away* (1992); *The Dreams of Mairhe Mehan: An Novel of the Civil War* (1996)

Avi, *The True Confessions of Charlotte Doyle* (1990); *Nothing But the Truth: A Documentary Novel* (1991), and others

Block, Francesca Lia, *Weetzie Bat* (1989); *Witch Baby* (1991); *Cherokee Bat and the Goat Guys* (1992); *Missing Angel Juan* (1993); *The Hanged Man* (1994); *Baby Be-Bop* (1995); *Girl Goddess #9: Nine Stories* (1996)

Blume, Judy, *Are You There God? It's Me, Margaret* (1970); *Then Again, Maybe I Won't* (1971); *Deenie* (1973); *Forever . . .* (1975); *Tiger Eyes* (1982); *Just as Long as We're Together* (1987); *Here's to You, Rachel Robinson* (1993), and others

Brooks, Bruce, *The Moves Make the Man* (1984); *Midnight Hour Encores* (1986); *No Kidding* (1989); *Everywhere* (1990); *What Hearts* (1992); *Asylum for Nightface* (1996), and others

Bunting, Eve, *Spying on Miss Müller* (1995)

Cooney, Caroline B., *The Face on the Milk Carton* (1990)

Cormier, Robert, *The Chocolate War* (1974); *I Am the Cheese* (1977); *After the First Death* (1979); *In the Middle of the Night* (1995); *Tenderness* (1997), and others

Creech, Sharon, *Absolutely Normal Chaos* (1995)

Crutcher, Chris, *Running Loose* (1983); *Stotan!* (1986); *Athletic Shorts* (1991); *Staying Fat for Sarah Byrnes* (1993); *Ironman* (1995)

Duncan, Lois, *I Know What You Did Last Summer* (1973); *Killing Mr. Griffin* (1978); *Don't Look Behind You* (1989); *Who Killed My Daughter?* (1992), and others

Farmer, Nancy, *The Ear, the Eye and the Arm* (1994); *A Girl Named Disaster* (1996), and other books for younger readers

Fine, Anne, *Alias Madame Doubtfire* (1988); *My War with Goggle Eyes The Book of the Banshee* (1992); *Flour Babies* (1994); *Step by Wicked Step* (1996); *The Tulip Touch* (1997), and others

Fleischman, Paul, *Joyful Noise: Poems for Two Voices*, illustrated by Eric Beddows (1988); *A Fate Totally Worse Than Death* (1995); *Seedfolks*, illustrated by Judy Pedersen (1997), and others

Fox, Paula, *The Eagle Kite* (1995)

Frank, Lucy, *I Am an Artichoke* (1995)

Garden, Nancy, *Annie on My Mind* (1982); *Dove and Sword: A Novel of Joan of Arc* (1995); *Good Moon Rising* (1996), and others

Hamilton, Virginia, *The House of Dies Drear* (1968); *The Planet of Junior Brown* (1971); *M. C. Higgins, the Great* (1974), *Plain City* (1993), and others

Hesse, Karen, *Letters from Rifka* (1992); *Phoenix Rising* (1994); *A Time of Angels* (1995); *The Music of Dolphins* (1996), and others

Hinton, S. E., *The Outsiders* (1967); *Tex* (1980); *Taming of the Star Runner* (1988), and others

Hobbs, Will, *Bearstone* (1989); *Downriver* (1991); *The Big Wander* (1992); *Far North* (1996); *River Thunder* (1997), and others

Kerr, M. E., *Dinky Hocker Shoots Smack!* (1972); *If I Love You, Am I Trapped Forever?* (1973); *Night Kites* (1986); *Deliver Us From Evie* (1994); *"Hello," I Lied* (1997), and others

Krisher, Trudy, *Spite Fences* (1994)

Lasky, Kathryn, *The Bone Wars* (1988); *Beyond the Burning Time* (1994); *Memoirs of a Bookbat* (1994), and others

Lipsyte, Robert, *The Contender* (1967); *One Fat Summer* (1977); *Summer Rules* (1981); *The Summerboy* (1982); *The Brave* (1991); *The Chemo Kid* (1992); *The Chief* (1993), and others

Lynch, Chris, *Shadow Boxer* (1993); *Iceman* (1994); *Gypsy Davey* (1994); *Slot Machine* (1995); *Blue-Eyed Son Trilogy: Blood Relations; Dog Eat Dog; Mick* (1996); *Political Timber* (1996), and others

Myers, Walter Dean, *Fast Sam, Cool Clyde, and Stuff* (1975); *It Ain't All for Nothin'* (1978); *The Young Landlords* (1979); *Motown and Didi* (1984); *Somewhere in the Darkness* (1992); *The Glory Field* (1994); *Darnell Rock Reporting* (1994); *Slam!* (1996), and others

Nelson, Theresa, *Earthshine* (1994)

Paulsen, Gary, *Dancing Carl* (1983); *Hatchet* (1987); *The Crossing* (1987); *The Winter Room* (1989); *Woodsong* (1990); *Canyons* (1990); *The Haymeadow* (1992); *Harris and Me: A Summer Remembered* (1993); *Brian's Winter* (1996), and others

Peck, Richard, *The Ghost Belonged to Me* (1975); *Ghosts I Have Been* (1977); *The Dreadful Future of Blossom Culp* (1983); *Father Figure* (1978); *Secrets of the Shopping Mall* (1979); *Princess Ashley* (1987); *The Last Safe Place on Earth* (1995), and others

Pullman, Philip, *The Ruby in the Smoke* (1987); *The Shadow in the North* (1988); *The Tiger in the Well* (1990); *The Broken Bridge* (1992); *The Golden Compass* (1996); *The Subtle Knife* (1997), and others

Rodowsky, Colby, *Julie's Daughter* (1985); *Lucy Peale* (1992); *Hannah In Between* (1994); *Sydney, Invincible* (1995); *Remembering Mog* (1996), and others

Vail, Rachel, *Do-Over* (1992); *Ever After* (1994); *Wonder* (1991); *Daring to be Abigail* (1996)

van Dijk, Lutz, *Damned Strong Love: The True Story of Willi G. and Stefan K.* (1995)

Voigt, Cynthia, *Homecoming* (1981); *Dicey's Song* (1982); *A Solitary Blue* (1984); *Seventeen Against the Dealer* (1989); *Orfe* (1992); *The Wings of a Falcon* (1993); *When She Hollers* (1994); *Bad Girls* (1996), and others

Walsh, Jill Paton, *Fireweed* (1969); *Unleaving* (1976); *A Chance Child* (1978); *Grace* (1992), and others

Wittlinger, Ellen, *Lombardo's Law* (1993)

Wolff, Virginia Euwer, *Make Lemonade* (1993)

And . . .

Web site for the American Library Association
http://www.ala.org/

Part Two

Reflections, Opinions, Prescriptions

The Lure of the Library

I love the library. Sometimes I find myself stopping to catch my breath as I enter a public library. All those books, magazines, newspapers, and people willing to help me — and in this country, it's free! I can easily spend more time than I have when I visit the library, yet I never regret it. A quest for an article in a magazine may yield not only the facts I need to help write a stronger letter to the city council, but also unexpected insights from browsing through other periodicals. What a treasure!

My affection for the library began at an early age. I loved thumbing through the card catalog for books and authors I thought I would like to read. Yet by the time I was nine or ten, I had read all the children's books in our tiny branch library except for those that tended to end with the death of the main character — usually a dog or a horse. I was tired of animal stories that made me cry. I wanted to read stories about girls like me, or biographies of baseball players, or Helen Keller or Abraham Lincoln. There was no library at my elementary school and my allowance would pay for only so many paperbacks from school book clubs (that, and candy). This lack of fresh material might have caused me to stop reading for fun, had my mother not decided to make regular field trips to the main library, with its immense collection of endless possibilities. I didn't have to read all the books, but I felt better knowing they were all there.

The fastest and undoubtedly the most charming way to get to the main library in Newport Beach, California, across the bay from our home in Corona del Mar, was on the Balboa Ferry — three cars to a boat, twenty-five-cent toll. Thinking about it, I can still smell gasoline from the motorboat gas station, hear the long and deep "Hoo" of the ferry's horn, see the sails of small boats blowing in the breeze, and feel the ferry bump as it pulls into the dock on the other side of the bay. On the return trip we often stopped on Balboa Island for a frozen banana covered with melted chocolate and dipped in rainbow sprinkles. No wonder I was glad my books had to be returned every two weeks.

By taking me to the library, my mother showed me that she valued reading and also that she valued me. I was important, my needs mattered. We talked in the car. Our trips were an adventure and a joy. I wish every child could experience a library on the other side of a ferryboat ride.

When I was in junior high, my father's job took us to the San Fernando Valley in Los Angeles. It was a turbulent time (1966) and place to be a teen. Fortunately I made a couple of close friends, but I carpooled with two sisters who stumbled into the car each morning with hair teased up to the ceiling, wearing miniskirts not much longer than the belts on their hips and stockings with at least three runs on each leg. (When I first met them, the older girl stuck her nose in the air and said, "Our father works in Hollywood.") Drugs were dealt and used routinely on campus, and school officials seemed oblivious.

The library was my refuge. After school a few days a week, Mom drove me to the library on the other side of the Ventura Freeway (which wasn't exactly the Balboa Ferry, but I took what I could get under the circumstances). Away from the radio and the telephone, I was able to do my homework and have time left over to browse. I remember searching for

John Updike books after reading one of his stories in Sunday School. I thought perhaps his writings might be a little too "adult" for me, so I never brought his books home. I simply read and enjoyed them all to myself, then surreptitiously returned them to the shelves.

High school found us on the other side of the country in Greenwich, Connecticut, where the bathrooms in the old high school were filled with cigarette smoke and the library stood on the corner of the Boston Post Road and a tree-lined — and sometimes snow-covered — street. My family lived five miles out of town, so my brother Brent drove me to school and to the library until I got my own driver's license. Swamped as I was with academics and after-school activities, I convinced myself that I didn't have time to read. But when I needed old magazines and newspapers for my social studies report on the Cuban Missile Crisis, or *Scientific American* articles for biology class, my friends at the library were there to help me.

I could actually *walk* to the library when I was a student at Stanford University. Once, after a particularly long study session in the stacks during finals, I emerged from my carrel around midnight to check out a book. Noticing a small bin of paper at the stand where I filled out my card, I looked more closely to read: "SCRATCH PAPER." Below the label a student had carefully penciled the addendum: "if it itches." I laughed out loud right there, and smiled all the way back to my dorm. Finals weren't so bad after all.

Now I am a mother, and one of the things I have consciously decided is to do everything I can to plant and nurture the seeds that I hope will grow into my daughters' lifelong love of the library. In Palo Alto, it's pretty easy. We're fortunate to have a library that's just for children — where the librarians have dedicated their careers to children's books and children's literacy, where there is a wooden carousel horse to climb on by the front door, a Secret Garden out back, and a built-in step for little ones at the checkout counter. I've let my kids pull books out for themselves from the time they were old enough to walk. We attended story hours when they were preschoolers, and took part in the summer reading program as they were beginning to read, at a time when every book completed was worthy of public celebration. If Allison needs a book on squirrels or California missions, we pile into my car and drive to the library. Only a few years ago she was looking for the pretty pictures; now she can use the computer to find resources she needs for school reports. I consider that a cause for private celebration. And if we somehow can't find what we need from the computer, we ask one of the librarians. They're always there, and they know so much.

Some of our favorite books were library finds. If we've checked out a book three or more times, I'll look for it in a bookstore. If we're lucky, it won't be out of print. Even some of the most charming picture books published in the last several years are no longer available because publishers have discontinued them. Thank goodness for libraries. And my only hope for rereading old favorites such as Evelyn Sibley Lampman's *Rusty's Space Ship* is at the you-know-what. At least once a year I drive to nearby Mountain View to another library I like, which wisely has held onto two copies of this fantasy tale. I can also get it through interlibrary loan, another magnificent service.

My first stop at our library is the new books section. I read the book reviews, so I know that the books the librarians are choosing to buy, especially in these lean times, are the best of the bunch. Holding and reading a brand-new library book is one of life's pure and simple pleasures. And it doesn't cost a dime.

Libraries are also wonderful when kids can't get enough of a favorite author or series. After Jennifer read two of Lois Lowry's "Anastasia" books when she was in the hospital recovering from food poisoning, she just *had* to have the rest. They were at the library. Or when Molly proudly read by herself her very first book, *Ten Apples Up On Top!* (which she had checked out of the school library), she wanted every Theo. LeSieg (aka Dr. Seuss) title she could get her hands on. They were waiting for us on the shelves of the library.

We have special, designated places in our family room for Children's Library books and school library books. The system must work, for we haven't lost any yet. We have been charged a few fines in our time, yet it's a small price to pay for the pleasures we've received. Actually, I put the Friends of the Library right up there near the top of my charitable causes.

Some authors get their biggest thrill when they first see their book in a bookstore. For me it was finding myself listed on the library computer. I was not just in the library, I was *in* the library, in the card catalog! I still look up my name and the listing of my book, *When Molly Was in the Hospital,* every time I go into the public library. (My kids tease me about leaving the citation on the computer when I leave.) Palo Alto has three copies; I like to see how many of my babies are checked out.

One summer day while in New York for a conference, I decided to take the train out to visit Greenwich and donate copies of my book to the town's library and hospital. I hadn't been back in fifteen years (my parents returned to California when I was in college). I wondered, would I recognize the town? Greenwich Avenue was where I remembered it, but almost all the stores were new. Many were the same as in downtown Palo Alto or Stanford Shopping Center. Ah, but there was still a cop directing traffic across from the Greenwich Post Office. Some things never change.

I took a detour over a block to the old high school, now the new and remodeled town hall. That *had* changed! I stood in the foyer, painfully recalling how lost I had felt on that spot my first day of school in 1968. "I used to go to high school here," I confessed to the receptionist.

"So did I," she replied. "It's a lot nicer now, isn't it?"

"I'll say." I had to check out a bathroom: delightfully smoke-free.

Leaving the old high school, I wandered up the side street I thought led to the library. It did. The town hall had been deserted at noon on this hot and humid July Monday, but the library was packed. I was impressed. And even though it, too, was remodeled, I felt right at home. Before I could find the Information desk to drop off a copy of my book, I saw the computers. Hmmm . . .

Their system was quite similar to Palo Alto's. I chose to do an "Author" search. "Duncan, Debbie" I typed, then punched Return.

In a split second, the familiar citation appeared on the screen: "Duncan, Debbie. When Molly was in the hospital: a book for brothers and sisters of hospitalized children."

Greenwich Library had bought my book! The librarians had chosen *my* book for their collection. Sure, it had gotten a glowing review in *School Library Journal* (and that's undoubtedly where the librarians had heard about it), but that wasn't nearly as thrilling as knowing one of my old libraries had actually purchased a book I had written. I was so excited when I introduced myself to the gracious woman at the Information desk and told her my story. She gladly accepted another, signed copy of the book. I was a happy camper. I had made it in the world.

The library can be an exciting place for anyone, not just aspiring or newly published authors. Be a caring parent and take your child to the library. If you work during the day, go on the weekend. Get library cards for everyone. Learn how to use the computer. Know your local librarian. Ask for help when you need it; I always do. Support the public library and the school library with donations, volunteer time, and, if necessary, letters to local and state legislators for increased funding for libraries and librarians. They deserve it, because we deserve the best libraries. Make sure your children know that the library is important to your family and the community at large.

Children who make friends with the library have a friend for life, no matter where in this country their lives may take them. ❦

Books

Duncan, Debbie, *When Molly Was in the Hospital: A Book for Brothers and Sisters of Hospitalized Children*, illustrated by Nina Ollikainen, MD (1994)

Lampman, Evelyn Sibley, *Rusty's Space Ship* (1957)

LeSieg, Theo., *Ten Apples Up On Top!*, illustrated by Roy McKie (1961)

The Reading Diet

child who loves the written word will most likely grow up reading a variety of materials in addition to books: newspapers, magazines, cereal boxes, notes and letters, the Internet and other items on the computer, TV listings, Sunday comics, box scores, game instructions, crossword puzzles, hymnals, sheet music, billboards, theater programs, titles on movie screens, recipes, catalogs, street signs, whatever. I'll never forget the marvelous feeling of being able to read — really read words! — and wanting to read everything around me. California still posts the signs I tried to figure out at age six (SPEED CHECKED BY RADAR). "What does 'speed chick-ed by ruh-dar?' mean, Mom?" I asked.

In the best of all scenarios, children also should read from a broad scope of genres, or types of books: realistic fiction, historical fiction, histories, biographies, fantasy, fairy tales, science fiction, animal stories, short stories, sports stories, mysteries, poetry, plays, arts and crafts books, drawing books, science project books, cookbooks, animal care books, series books, joke books, and comic books. As much as I believe children should read great books (there are so many out there!), I also feel that a little junk in a well-balanced reading diet is perfectly fine.

When I was about ten, I used to grab the evening paper as soon as it was delivered so I could read Ann Landers. I still read the comics every day, and look forward to catching up on celebrity gossip in *People* magazine when I get my hair cut. For a while I read every Amanda Cross mystery I could find, and I still recommend Joy Fielding's *See Jane Run* to my women friends who want an exciting, page-turning read. (I did, however, give up Danielle Steel about fifteen years ago. The best thing she ever wrote, as far as I'm concerned, was her contribution to the group prenatal guide, *Having a Baby*.)

I consider myself a well-rounded reader. The first book of *Anna Karenina* remains my favorite novel, and I long to savor its passion again. In the meantime, I try to read the cover story in the *New York Times Magazine* every Sunday. I've discovered some fabulous writers in the *Times*: Anna Quindlen, Jane Brody, Molly O'Neill, and the sports writers who covered the Yankees in the World Series. I try not to miss the My Turn column in *Newsweek*. A couple of Wallace Stegner paperbacks sit on my bedside table, waiting for my summer vacation, along with Arthur Miller's *The Crucible* (the play, not the movie) and Gina Beriault's *Women in Their Beds*. I read children's books — lots of them.

My parents are readers. When I was growing up, Mom always seemed to have a paperback book in her hand — while she heated baby formula, sunbathed, or waited in the car to pick up one or more of her four children. We had *Time*, *Life*, and *National Geographic* on our family room coffee table. I was raised on the *Los Angeles Times*. To this day my father studies poetry and Shakespeare, yet he also read and enjoyed Bette Bao Lord's adult novel about China, *Spring Moon*. Many years later I was able to share with Dad Lord's fictionalized account of the year she emigrated from China, *In the Year of the Boar and Jackie Robinson*. This affectionate portrayal of a Chinese girl trying to fit in in 1947 Brooklyn is one of my favorite children's books.

I know my younger brother missed reading the comics when we moved to Greenwich, and the *New York Times* became our daily paper. So what did twelve-year-old Dwight do? Used his allowance to subscribe to one of the tabloid papers that did have comics. My parents never complained he was wasting his money; they just read their paper as he read his at the breakfast table every morning. It's an image I have in my mind that I wish now we had captured on film.

The dean of admissions at Stanford announced proudly to my graduating class that *his* favorite book was *The Phantom Tollbooth*, Norton Juster's extraordinarily clever fantasy about Milo's adventures in the lands of Dictionopolis and Digitopolis and his quest to accomplish the impossible — rescue the banished princesses Rhyme and Reason from the Castle in the Air so that everyone in the kingdom can get along. This modern classic and perennial best seller somehow eluded me in the 1960s (perhaps adults in California considered it only a New York phenomenon because it has illustrations by the cartoonist Jules Feiffer). I have Dean Fred to thank for inspiring me to read it as an adult. It's a tale brimming with wit, wisdom, and plays on words. It is indeed a book for all ages. I couldn't wait to read it to my children when I felt they were old enough to begin to appreciate it. Third grade?

"Can we read something else?" Jennifer said one night, shaking her head after a couple of chapters. "I don't get it."

Sigh. "All right," I replied, reaching for a Beverly Cleary.

But wait! A few months later, Jennifer had a chance to try out for the play *The Phantom Tollbooth* at Palo Alto Children's Theatre. Cast as "The Map" as well as a Spelling Bee, Jennifer read the script straight through the day she received her copy. "Now I understand," she said. "This is great!" Before the seven performances were over she had not only memorized everyone's lines (except, most understandably, the boy's that included a letter written entirely in four-digit numbers), she also went back to read the entire book to herself.

Reading the story in a different form — a play — had helped her understand it. This happened with Allison as well. Her first role was Minnie Mae in Palo Alto Children's Theatre's musical adaptation of L. M. Montgomery's *Anne of Green Gables*. Allison was only in second grade, but every day at school she read from her two-inch-thick paperback copy of *Anne*. In another instance, we had received a beautiful collection of Beatrix Potter books as a birth present for Allison, but the girls had never taken to them until Jennifer played Tabitha Twitchit on stage. Suddenly the set of books was read, enjoyed, and argued over by my older daughters. Enjoyment and appreciation of plays based on fairy tales and great works of literature extend beyond the performers, of course. Children in the audience are frequently inspired to read the original works or hear them read aloud after viewing the play in the Theatre. This is also why audio books are popular with younger *and* older children. Some children learn better by listening.

I like to see children approaching literature and learning from several angles. Parents should pay attention to what works for their child, capitalize on it, and then . . . vary it. Expand the diet, if you will. Kids who spend hours surfing the Internet should also read books. Children (such as mine) who have a decided preference for fiction can also enjoy looking through *The World Almanac for Kids* or *Guinness Record Breakers*. Kids who like *Babe*, the movie, should go back and read *Babe*, the book by Dick King-Smith. Children who are addicted to "Goosebumps" may not know that they are actually hooked on reading. Suggest they read a story that virtually every kid falls in love with, Susan Cooper's *The Boggart*, and see what happens.

Or maybe do as I did one Christmas and buy Bill Watterson's *The Calvin and Hobbes Tenth Anniversary Book* for your child. This splendid comic strip, alas, is no longer available in the daily papers, but the collection delighted ten-year-old Jennifer for days on end. At the same time she was engrossed in a historical novel, Elizabeth George Speare's

The Witch of Blackbird Pond, for school reading. Two completely different books and reading experiences. Both part of my child's complete reading diet. 🍎

Books

Cooper, Susan, *The Boggart* (1993)

Juster, Norton, *The Phantom Tollbooth*, illustrated by Jules Feiffer (1961)

King-Smith, Dick, *Babe: The Gallant Pig*, illustrated by Mary Rayner (1985)

Lord, Bette Bao, *In the Year of the Boar and Jackie Robinson*, illustrated by Marc Simont (1984)

Montgomery, L. M., *Anne of Green Gables* (1908)

Potter, Beatrix, *The Tale of Peter Rabbit* (1902)

Speare, Elizabeth George, *The Witch of Blackbird Pond* (1958)

Watterson, Bill, *The Calvin and Hobbes Tenth Anniversary Book* (1995)

The World Almanac for Kids (1997)

Young, Karen Romano, *Guinness Record Breakers* (1997)

Those Reading Lists

I have mixed feelings whenever I hear that a book I enjoy has been added to a required reading list. On the one hand, I'm delighted. Books used in the classroom are guaranteed longer print lives. (We authors especially appreciate this.) Well-written children's books can teach history, science, social studies — many subjects besides English. And yet, I also can't help thinking, Uh-oh, there goes the book. It's ruined. It will be dissected to death, or remembered as punishment, and no kid will ever enjoy it again.

Literature was not used in teaching reading when I was young. I started with "Dick and Jane" in first grade, and progressed to anthologies of unremarkable stories all the way until the end of junior high. School reading was easy but uninteresting. (Home reading was the fun stuff.) On the first day of tenth-grade English, however, my literary education began with George Eliot's *Silas Marner*. By the time we finished three months later, Richard Nixon and Spiro Agnew had won the '68 election, and I was bored beyond belief. Three months for one novel! Until then I thought I had *liked* reading and had had dreams of majoring in English in college. But if that meant endless rounds of stop and start, of painstaking analysis and dissection, I'd find another major, thank you very much.

There was just one book that I adored in high school (other than *Gone With the Wind*, that is). Over one October weekend during my junior year, I was assigned to read the first chapter of Harper Lee's Pulitzer Prize-winning novel, *To Kill a Mockingbird*. October weekends in Connecticut in 1969 meant raking and burning leaves. I volunteered to sit on a log in the middle of the back yard and supervise the pile of burning leaves while my brothers and parents (bless them!) raked, piled, and brought leaves to my post. I also read *To Kill a Mockingbird*. The whole thing. My teacher didn't tell me I *couldn't* finish it, so I did because I couldn't put it down. I read it before the inevitable vocabulary lists, essay questions, pop quizzes, or tests could ruin it for me. I always think of *To Kill a Mockingbird* on those rare days in Northern California when I catch a whiff of burning Autumn leaves.

Now literature is used in classrooms beginning in kindergarten. When taught well, good books can motivate as well as educate. Our family never would have known about Judi and Ron Barrett's unique picture book, *Cloudy With a Chance of Meatballs*, if it hadn't been second grade core literature in our district. What a silly, clever way for students to learn about the weather! Books in the classroom are absolutely necessary for children who aren't being read to at home.

But why does it have to take months for a fourth-grade class to read Scott O'Dell's Newbery Award-winning survival story, *Island of the Blue Dolphins*? By the time the kids finish analyzing and writing and tearing the book apart word by word and chapter by chapter, many students — strong readers, weak readers, and all those in-between — just want to get rid of the darn thing. Thinking about another book, Jennifer observed two years after the fact, "I loved *By the Great Horn Spoon* when you read it to me. But when we studied it in school, I couldn't stand it!"

What can parents do? Don't think your job as reading coach is finished if your child's school uses literature in the classroom. Children should always have a good book going simultaneously, whether you are reading it to them or they're reading it to themselves. Kids who grow up in households where reading is an enjoyable and predictable part of daily life are less likely to be turned off to reading when they are bored by equating books only with schoolwork.

Find out what your children will be assigned to read (this may not apply to the early elementary grades in all schools). There should be a list of core literature by grade level. Read these books yourself, maybe even a year or two ahead of time. If you think your child would enjoy hearing them, read them aloud. My children study E. B. White's well-told (if old-fashioned) love story, *The Trumpet of the Swan*, in fourth grade, but I've read it to Allison and Molly when they were six or seven. First graders are especially able to identify with Louis the voiceless swan when he goes to school to learn how to read and write, just as they do every day.

From the Mixed-Up Files of Mrs. Basil E. Frankweiler (the titles of E. L. Konigsburg's books always crack me up, even if I don't always remember them verbatim) remains one of my all-time favorite children's books, full of adventure — in the Metropolitan Museum of Art, no less — mystery, humor, a delightful brother and sister team, and an eccentric old lady. I read it to Jennifer two years before she had to answer seven essay questions a week and spend a weekend drawing an object from the Met. (Thank goodness no one ever asks *me* to draw any more.) What was her final verdict? "Still a good book." In the hands of a gifted fifth-grade teacher, the story held its charm.

Parents cannot depend entirely on teachers to bring literature alive, even in the best schools. Read great books to your children, and, once they are able, also encourage them to read for pleasure. For fun. No questions asked and no lists kept. Not to please you or any other adult. Read for themselves.

Make sure there is a plentiful supply of books you think your child would enjoy, and let him choose. If he doesn't like a certain one, he doesn't have to finish it. If she wants to read a book four times over or read two or three at a time, she can do it. That's the way children learn the joy of reading.

During the summer before Jennifer began sixth grade, we received a huge mailing from the middle school she would be entering in the fall. I, of course, zeroed in on the letter from the school librarian, along with a suggested summer reading list and reading contest. "Look at this, Jennifer. You've already read many of these books — *The Boggart, The Midwife's Apprentice, Yolanda's Genius.* All you have to do is write 'em down and write a paragraph about one of them. There'll be a special party in September for all the students who participate."

My daughter looked at the paper with its sea of blank lines and shook her head. "I don't want to do a summer reading list," she announced.

I took a deep breath and . . . didn't say anything. I didn't say that listing all the books she'd read would be a good way to show her new teacher and librarian what a strong reader she is. (I also didn't say that listing the books would be a good way to show her new teacher and librarian what a good parent I am.) I left the sheet out on the kids' junk table in the kitchen, and asked her once more (okay, maybe twice more) before school started if she wanted to write down the books she'd read over the summer. The answer was always no.

As luck would have it, my first hour of volunteering at the middle school library was during the party for the students who had turned in a summer reading list. I handed out prizes and help serve pizza and soft drinks. "Why isn't Jennifer here?" one of her good friends wanted to know.

"I think it had something to do with writing that paragraph," I said.

Jennifer looked only slightly sheepish that afternoon. "They didn't say it would be a *pizza* party," she lamented.

"Do you think you'll keep track of your reading next summer so you can go to next year's pizza party?"

She thought for a moment. "Will I have to write about a book?"

"I don't know. Not everyone did who was invited to the party today. Writing a paragraph would probably take you about five minutes."

"Hmmm. I think I'll do it," she said. "But I'll decide next summer."

As long as she's reading, I told myself. As long as she's still reading. 🍎

Books

Barrett, Judi, *Cloudy With a Chance of Meatballs*, illustrated by Ron Barrett (1978)

Cooper, Susan, *The Boggart* (1993)

Cushman, Karen, *The Midwife's Apprentice* (1995)

Fenner, Carol, *Yolanda's Genius* (1995)

Fleischman, Sid, *By the Great Horn Spoon*, illustrated by Eric von Schmidt (1963)

Konigsburg, E. L., *From the Mixed-Up Files of Mrs. Basil E. Frankweiler* (1967)

Lee, Harper, *To Kill a Mockingbird* (1960)

O'Dell, Scott, *Island of the Blue Dolphins* (1960)

White, E. B., *The Trumpet of the Swan*, illustrated by Edward Frascino (1970)

Turning Sick Time into Reading Time

One fall Saturday morning, six-year-old Molly awoke with a nasty virus. Her breakfast ended up on the kitchen floor and her face turned as white as our countertop. She barely had the energy to be cleaned up and escorted to the couch. After writing all week, I had so many plans for my weekend — baking, laundry, shopping, walking the dog — plans that evaporated when I knew I had a sick kid. Illness has a way of doing that.

Bill stayed with Molly while I zipped through my essential errands. He had made up a particularly cozy sickbed in the family room by the time I returned to settle down next to her to read. The first book I picked up from the stack of Halloween books on the coffee table was a little long, I decided. "But wait," I said. "We have all day, don't we?"

Indeed we did. And that, of course, is the opportunity illness offers parents and children, and usually without notice. For parents, it's the chance to stop and give more than the customary amount of attention to our kids. To read or play quiet games or activities with a child who stays still longer than usual. To offer comfort. For children, it's a chance to absorb all that love and attention, lousy as they may feel.

That day we went through all our Halloween books and then some. If she had been slightly older we probably would have started and finished a chapter book, if she had felt up to paying attention that long. Jennifer and Allison stopped by to listen or to help read to their sister while I folded a load of laundry or sliced bagels. Some chores absolutely had to be done, so I made a deal with Molly: even without reinforcements, I took a break after every two or three books to accomplish a task. She thought that was fair and used the time to arrange clips in her doll's hair.

Even though I work at home, I'm never able to write when I have a sick child. For that I need long, uninterrupted stretches of time, time that just isn't there when a feverish child is down the hall. When Molly was *really* sick at a year and a half, I was so preoccupied and worried that I didn't write at all for three months. After her successful diagnosis during her third hospitalization, I wrote an essay about our ordeal, and it was published as a My Turn column in *Newsweek*. I have an enormous amount of empathy and respect for parents of severely or chronically ill children who have to quit work in order to care for their kids.

Our family has spent more than its fair share of time in the hospital. And yet, looking back, there were actually plusses to those experiences. I recall one afternoon hastily packing one of Jennifer's beloved books, Lois Lowry's *All About Sam*, when she had to be hospitalized for severe food poisoning. Later that night, I was reading my fearful and wan ten-year-old to sleep with a book she had read to herself at least a dozen times. Tethered to an IV pole through a tube in her foot, my normally active, independent child quietly listened to me read the familiar story about the early years of Sam Krupnik. "More," she mumbled when I finished the next morning.

"Just a minute," I replied. "I have an idea." I padded down the hall in my stockinged feet to the hospital's Family Library, where to my delight I found on the book cart two other stories about the Krupnik family, *Anastasia at Your Service* and *Anastasia's Chosen Career*. By the time we finished them the following day, Jennifer was unhooked from her IV and ready to go home. She was hungry for food — and more Anastasia books.

Allison had her appendix out the next summer, and while most of her thirty hours in the hospital were spent in surgery or recovering from the operation, we read two of Judy Blume's books about Peter and Fudge, *Tales of a Fourth Grade Nothing* and *Superfudge*, while she was confined to bed. When Allison was home sick for several days during third grade with a low-grade something — not ill enough to stay in bed, but not well enough to go to school, I decided to use the time to read a book to myself that I had just heard about, Rodman Philbrick's *Freak the Mighty*.

"Can you read it to me?" Allison asked.

"I don't know," I said honestly. "It's supposed to be about two eighth-grade boys, one big and brainless, the other small and smart. It's for older kids and it might be kind of sad. Would you really like to hear it?"

"Uh-huh," she said. "Please?"

So I did something I don't usually do, which was to read a book above my child's level that I hadn't read first. Fortunately, Allison was able to handle a kidnapping, a nonviolent death, and quite a bit of meanness on the sidelines. I don't think I could have at her age, but all children are different. *Freak the Mighty* was serious, but it was also compelling and funny. Allison fell in love with the main characters. She and I were able to talk about them while the house was quiet, and report our impressions at the dinner table when the rest of the family gathered together. She returned to school the next week wiser for having spent time with Freak and Max. And she felt *so* grown-up in fourth grade when she visited the library with a friend and found *Freak the Mighty* in the Young Adult section. She checked it out, and kept it in her desk to read to herself at school. My gamble paid off.

Sick days can also be an opportune time for older children to tackle books they might not normally get around to reading. Without classes or after-school obligations competing for time, a novel doesn't seem so long. Jennifer read E. L. Konigsburg's 1997 Newbery Award winner, *The View from Saturday*, while sick at home during sixth grade. The five main characters — four sixth graders and their teacher/Academic Bowl coach — are fascinating and compelling, but their stories are clearer if they can be read in one sitting.

I've used reading to entertain and distract my children when they were stressed or worried. In the days immediately following the Loma Prieta earthquake in 1989, I read all of our picture books several times over to Jennifer and Allison, who were four and two years old. They refused to leave the house, even though that's where they were when the earthquake crashed through our home, buckling the floor and upsetting our lives (along with quite a few breakables). A couple of years later, a fire in the nearby foothills forced us to postpone Jennifer's half-birthday sleepover party. While we were fairly certain we were going to be safe, we did start loading photo albums into the car when we realized our home was between the flames and the hastily posted notice about the Red Cross shelter. The fire danger passed, but still Jennifer was incredibly upset and disappointed. Books helped us get through that scary night. And the next evening, we had the party after all.

Humor is especially helpful when kids are anxious. There is one chapter in Eleanor Estes's *Ginger Pye* that I pull out to reread when my children need a dose of the giggles. In "Ginger on the Fire Escape," Ginger the dog desperately wants to find out where his master, Jerry, goes every day. In trailing Jerry Pye's scent to school, Ginger gets gravel up his nose, forgets his quest and fights with a cat, remembers what he's supposed to do, finds Jerry's pencil, and pushes it all the way to a big brick building. Ginger wonders why Jerry would want to spend every day in a place like this? Finding no open doors, he dozes in the sun until he hears Jerry's voice coming from one of the high windows. Energized, Ginger climbs carefully up the iron staircase, pencil in mouth. When the dog triumphantly reaches the window sill, Jerry is reading a report about . . . Ginger! Everyone in the room except for the tall one, "the person in command," is delighted to see Ginger, the dog who's smart enough to trail Jerry to school and bring a pencil with him.

Ginger Pye was awarded the Newbery Medal in 1952. In addition to getting the dog's point of view down perfectly, Eleanor Estes provides modern children with an excellent representation of American life around 1920. My kids are glad their teachers and classrooms are *nothing* like Jerry Pye's. And while the author frequently strays, like her main character does while trailing his master, from the main story of Ginger's eventual kidnapping, *Ginger Pye* is worth reading and rereading aloud for its humor and endearing characters.

While it's no fun for anyone when kids are sick, reading can make those days seem not quite as dreary or interminable. It can even make them memorable. 🍎

Books

Blume, Judy, *Tales of a Fourth Grade Nothing*, illustrated by Roy Doty (1972); *Superfudge* (1980)

Estes, Eleanor, *Ginger Pye* (1951)

Konigsburg, E. L., *The View from Saturday* (1996)

Lowry, Lois, *All About Sam*, illustrated by Diane deGroat (1988); *Anastasia at Your Service* (1982); *Anastasia's Chosen Career* (1987)

Philbrick, Rodman, *Freak the Mighty* (1993)

What to Do About the (Ahem!) Television?

The simple answer is not to turn it on, especially in the evening. TV can't compete with more worthwhile indoor activities — reading, writing, homework, having a decent family conversation, or playing a game — if it isn't turned on. Parents need to make reading, not television, the primary after-dinner activity. If reading a good book is more interesting than watching whatever happens to be on television, TV need not be an issue.

I wish it were that easy. The fact is, TV is an issue, even in our household. My husband thinks of television as the ideal background noise. Bill would love to have a TV set in every room, including the bathrooms. He's still trying to figure out how to mount a hospital-style monitor in the kitchen so he can easily watch the news during dinner. Before retiring for the night, he perfects the sport of channel surfing on our bedroom set. During our family's two-week annual vacation in the mountains, Bill will read five or six novels to remind himself how much he enjoys reading. But back at home, his TV habit is hard to break.

I confess that I also have one or two programs I try to watch. I grew up on television, think the writing and acting on *Cheers* (the early years) were gifts to modern civilization, and while I could live without them, I enjoy watching *Frasier* or *Seinfeld* if I can fit them in after my younger ones are in bed. When Bill is traveling or working late, I have the family room TV on while preparing dinner; the folks behind the news desk remind me that I'm not the only adult in the world.

And then there is *Sesame Street*. I love *Sesame Street*. It's been a superb show for my children to grow up with, and I continue to turn it on occasionally in the late afternoon or on weekend mornings. It's one of those rare shows that educates and entertains children and adults alike. *Sesame Street* provides all young children who watch it a multicultural education of the highest caliber. No wonder it's still so popular with families. (Yes, I am aware that some early childhood educators find fault with the show, that its fast pace discourages attention span development. These experts prefer a quieter, slower show such as *Mister Rogers*. We tried *Mister Rogers*, but it was too soporific for us — we were all ready to take another nap after twenty minutes. Of course, that's not to say that other families don't enjoy *Mister Rogers* and benefit from it. I know that they do; we just don't happen to be among them. If my philosophy is to stop reading a book we don't care for, I'm certainly not going to turn on the television for a program my children don't like, just because it's supposed to be good for them.)

Reading Rainbow and *Storytime* are two wonderful PBS programs that are all about reading. Little ones enjoy them, and the shows also model good storytelling for parents. Watch these shows with your children, then turn off the TV and visit the library or bookstore if you want to get your hands on one of the featured books.

Arthur, the PBS program based on our family's favorite picture book series, is a newer show and a big hit with children up through elementary school. My girls were familiar with most of the stories that had already appeared in book form (which is good, because the library has had a hard time keeping the "Arthur" books on the shelf since the series premiered to wide acclaim and popularity), but the newer stories have a lot to offer, too. I even stopped making dinner one evening so I could pay closer attention to the ending of an episode dealing with book censorship. As is so often the case in real life, the parent who challenged the library books had not read them himself. "This is great stuff, guys," I said, and went on to explain to my daughters why I am opposed to any efforts to ban books.

I believe all children's television viewing should be supervised by parents. Are the programs your children wanting to watch really appropriate? Find out for yourself. How do you feel about TV violence? Watch and decide. Insist that your children don't just "watch TV," rather that they propose and watch a specific program. Take control of the television set and never let go.

Just as parents need to set limits on the amount of junk food their children eat, so they should limit the amount and type of television programming they consume. Milton Chen, PhD, author of the excellent and useful book, *The Smart Parent's Guide to Kids' TV*, recommends limiting children to two hours a day or less of television. (Children currently spend an average of four full hours a day in front of the TV.) I'd like my kids to watch a lot less than two hours a day, and in fact, during the week when homework, rehearsals, playing with friends, and reading are all part of the routine, they watch very little, if any, television. Jennifer's sixth-grade teacher told parents at back-to-school night, "I don't want my students watching *any* TV during the week. If there's a worthwhile science or history show on," Mr. Carothers continued, "tape it and watch it on the weekend. Make me the bad guy if you need to."

Mr. Carothers is the sort of bad guy teacher every child deserves. I agree: there is no real need to watch television during the week. After the news (which our children usually don't pay attention to, thank goodness, so they aren't exposed to the unnecessary calamities of real life), the TV is switched off as a matter of habit. The girls know that reading aloud is on the evening agenda, and they look forward to it. I haven't had to set a daily television limit (yet) because I've managed to make books the preferred activity. Kids control the pace with reading. They also have a wide variety of materials to choose from (not just those from Hollywood), and they aren't subjected to commercial overload. I don't think my children feel in the least bit deprived.

When Jennifer and Allison were little, we managed to convince them that channel 9 (the San Francisco PBS station) was the only one that came in on our TV. If they wanted to watch something else, it was on videotape. Even though Jennifer saw Saturday morning network cartoons at friends' houses during sleepovers, she didn't ask for them at home. Pandora's box was opened, however, when we discovered Nickelodeon in the hospital the week before she started fifth grade. As the girls soon found out, we did subscribe to Cable. I have to admit, Nickelodeon knows what kids like, and it's not bad stuff. *Rugrats* and *Doug* are clever, innovative programs. (Doug even keeps a journal and uses the library.) Too, I have enjoyed watching *I Love Lucy* reruns on Nickelodeon with Jennifer and Allison, both aspiring actresses. "Now *that's* acting!" I say. I'm also optimistic that the Federal Communications Commission mandate that TV stations carry three hours of educational programming each week (even three measly hours) will make more quality programs available for children.

So while TV isn't all bad, reading still beats television any day of the week. ❦

Book

Chen, Milton, *The Smart Parent's Guide to Kids' TV* (1994)

Summer Reading

I love summertime. I thrive on the longer days, the warmer weather, and the more relaxed pace of days that begin with big bowls of fruit from the Farmers Market. During my girls' early years, I searched for books set in the summer. We loved reading *Jesse Bear, What Will You Wear?* for Nancy White Carlstrom's cheerful verse and Bruce Degen's illustrations filled with a summertime feel. The first book Allison could read to herself, Leonard Kessler's *Last One In Is a Rotten Egg*, takes place in the hot days of summer and is about our favorite sport, swimming.

I'll never forget the summer day I arrived to pick Jennifer up from preschool, early enough to enjoy hearing the teacher read Cynthia Rylant and Stephen Gammell's Caldecott Honor winner, *The Relatives Came*. The book instantly brought back wonderful childhood memories of summer family reunions at my grandparents' Whittier home, when my favorite cousins from Washington state stayed for two weeks. Nancy and Jeanne shared the room that once was our mothers', and when I spent the night, I slept on the nearby sleeping porch. My aunt and uncle stayed in the guest room across the hall, and my boy cousins camped out in my other uncle's old bedroom. We all shared the same bathroom, with its blue, two-inch thick carpeting. Everywhere we turned, there were relatives. I was in heaven. *The Relatives Came* is a beautifully written, joyously illustrated picture book about a very large family reunion — the coming of the relatives, the chaos while they are here, and the emptiness when they leave. For years we've read it the night after my daughters' own cousins have left for home, when the house suddenly feels too empty.

Now that the children are older, I am among several in my household who appreciate having three months without homework on the evening agenda. Summer vacation means more time for free reading. The kids can play outside after dinner and still have time for an hour or two of reading, thanks to not having to get up at 7:00 in the morning. Jennifer and I dove into L. M. Montgomery's 1908 novel, *Anne of Green Gables*, the summer after Jennifer finished first grade. We wept our hearts out — in true Anne fashion — when Matthew Cuthbert died, and sobbed again at Anne's saying that ends the book: "God's in his heaven, all's right with the world." Jennifer the preteen will often read past midnight on summer nights.

Allison and I read another favorite about a strong female, Louise Fitzhugh's *Harriet the Spy*, the summer before she started fourth grade. I realized Allison was getting a little *too* much into the spying aspect of the story when I learned she was using her new binoculars to look into the window of a thirty-year-old neighbor and friend. Fortunately, Catherine laughed when she talked with Allison and me about it, for she, too, had been a real fan of *Harriet* as a young girl.

We find it easier to make weekly trips to the library during summer vacation; the kids are just too busy during the school year with after-school activities and homework to take the time for leisurely visits to the library. For several years Jennifer and Allison participated in the Children's Library summer reading program, keeping careful track of all the books we read. (Third child Molly somehow has missed out on that practice. I think her older sisters' aversion to list-keeping and their wish to read just for reading's sake has something to do with it.) I still have the summer reading brochure from the year Jennifer was seven and Allison five. Jennifer read (or was read to) 250; Allison, 101. No wonder Jennifer entered second grade reading some fifth- and sixth-grade-level titles. All that practice made her an avid, accomplished reader. Teachers and school administrators are constantly lamenting that children who don't read over the summer can lose reading skills, but I like to look at summer as an opportunity for kids to become *stronger* readers. So does my Pennsylvania friend, Catherine: when her middle school-age children, Leah and Josh, don't need to be ready for their summer activities until mid-morning, she wakes them up at 8:30 a.m. so they can have a leisurely hour to read in bed.

When we have more time for reading, I have more chances to listen to my children read aloud to me. I had heard scare stories from other (obsessive Baby Boomer) parents that kids were not learning how to read in first grade, that this whole language business so popular in California in the early 1990s meant that students checked books out from the library, then took them back to their desks in the classroom and just stared at them. Of course this was ludicrous, but I didn't know any better, so I enrolled Jennifer in a weekly reading program at the local community center the summer before she was to begin first grade. After the second session, one of the parents who had sat in on the class stopped me in the hallway. "When did your daughter learn to read?"

"Well," I stammered, balancing year-old Molly on my hip. "Pretty recently, I guess. She took her current favorite, *No Tooth, No Quarter!*, with her today to read aloud."

"She read the entire book to the class," the mother went on, "and with expression, too! She's way ahead of all the other children. I don't think she even needs this course."

What had happened is that the groundwork — yes, using whole language techniques — laid down by her talented kindergarten teacher, combined with the reading we did at home, made it easy for Jennifer to be able to read without any formal instruction in phonics. All those papers she scribbled on around the house and the labels we taped to objects, as well as the notes I wrote to her and the myriad books and magazines we made available, helped her figure out how to read the printed word. I realize this doesn't happen for all children, that many need phonics drills in order to become proficient readers. Yet if I had stopped worrying long enough to ask Jennifer to read to me, I would have saved $200 for the family, and Jennifer quite a few hours in a class she described as "boring."

Sometimes we take turns reading "parts" of picture books. One we use frequently, Marilyn Tolhurst and Simone Abel's *Somebody and the Three Blairs*, works well as a reader's theater. I'm usually assigned the part of the narrator in this amusing take on the Goldilocks story, where Somebody, the bear, visits the home of the Blair family while they are off in the park. ("Feeda ducks," says Baby Blair.) Ever since Molly started reading, she and Allison argue — er, decide politely — who gets to read the lines for the two kids' parts, Somebody and Baby Blair. ("This pond is too small," Somebody decides while looking into the toilet. And, "Issa big teddy bear," Baby Blair says when he finds Somebody sleeping in his crib.) On long summer evenings, we have time to switch parts and run it through again.

Bill, the family member who arises at 5:30 a.m. in winter *and* summer to walk the dog, read the papers, and go off to the office, occasionally will retire for the night before his daughters. If Molly or Allison realizes this, either may very well take one of their books into our bedroom and read Dad a story. Bill and I find this switch in roles quite touching.

Summer is also special to me because it brings our annual vacation at a family camp in the Sierra where no one has to get up for work. Early in August we make a pre-Camp field trip to local bookstores to load up on paperback oldies and hardcover irresistibles we'll have the time to indulge in over the two weeks. (Ever since I nearly ruined a library book by letting a damp beach towel get between its pages on a trip back from the lake, I discourage bringing books from the library on our vacation. We also inevitably lose something when we leave home, and I'd rather it not be a library book.) One bookstore has a huge table with summer reading suggestions from the schools in the area. Undoubtedly, I find a few treasures to purchase.

Our cabin at camp doesn't have a television or a telephone. During the day the girls hike, swim, or just hang out with other kids at the soda fountain. Bill devours the novels he's saved all year, as do I. I also sing in the a cappella group and visit with old friends. We take long walks and talk about jobs, books, children, hair, and life. After dinner, if there isn't an evening activity planned, we return to the cabin as a family to read or play games. I remember one year reading aloud the last book in Lynne Reid Banks's "Indian in the Cupboard" series, *The Mystery of the Cupboard*. Finally, we learned the origin of the magic of the cupboard that turned plastic figures into real, miniature people. It was such a satisfying ending to an unforgettable saga that had begun on the main character's birthday three books earlier.

A few years ago I served on our school district's calendar committee, charged with recommending school vacation days. Not surprisingly for a district digging up playgrounds to put in portable classrooms, the idea of year-round schooling came up. Selfishly, I cringed at the thought of losing our long, late-night warm-weather read-aloud time and our August vacation at camp. I wasn't alone, as a district-wide vote came down solidly in favor of tradition. Seems a lot of people in our town like summer the way it's always been.

And I hope it always will be. I do love summer. 🌢

Books

Banks, Lynne Reid, *The Mystery of the Cupboard*, illustrated by Tom Newsom (1993)

Buller, Jon and Susan Shade, *No Tooth, No Quarter!* (1989)

Carlstrom, Nancy White, *Jesse Bear, What Will You Wear?*, illustrated by Bruce Degen (1986)

179

Fitzhugh, Louise, *Harriet the Spy* (1964)

Kessler, Leonard, *Last One In Is a Rotten Egg* (1969)

Montgomery, L. M., *Anne of Green Gables* (1908)

Rylant, Cynthia, *The Relatives Came*, illustrated by Stephen Gammell (1985)

Tolhurst, Marilyn, *Somebody and the Three Blairs*, illustrated by Simone Abel (1991)

If You Are Inspired
To Write Children's Books . . .
This Is My Story

W e must have read at least five hundred picture books the summer after Jennifer finished kindergarten. One afternoon while making our way through another pile from the library, I announced to my kids, "Hey, I can write as well as most of these people. I think I'll write a children's book."

"What about, Mom?" six-year-old Jennifer asked.

"Um, I don't know. I'll have to think about it."

Which I did. The next month I started my first picture book manuscript, *One Week at Camp*, based on Jennifer's experience at our family camp near Lake Tahoe. Later that year I wrote a story inspired by a question I heard frequently from Allison: "What if I were an only child?" Where are those "books" now? In my file drawer — where they belong.

Before I could write a manuscript worthy of a publisher's investment, I needed to do more than write stories about cute or funny things my kids said, no matter how much they or their friends liked them. (And I was already a published essay writer.) First, I took a class taught by a local children's book author, JoAnne Stewart Wetzel. I went with a friend,

Rita, a fellow mom at Allison's preschool. It was fabulous. In one day JoAnne covered the basics of writing and submitting a children's book manuscript. Following her advice, I joined SCBWI, the Society of Children's Book Writers and Illustrators. SCBWI is the only professional organization solely for writers for children; its quarterly newsletter and continually updated lists of publishers are invaluable. I've attended meetings sponsored by our local chapter, and twice I made the trek to the annual national conference in Los Angeles, where I was inspired by the likes of Patricia MacLachlan, Lois Lowry, and Judy Blume, *and* rode the elevator with Louis Sachar.

JoAnne encouraged us to join a critique group (hers was closed, she informed us), where we could share our manuscripts. Through our local children's librarian, Rita heard about a potential writers group being organized by another author and writing teacher, SuAnn Kiser. SuAnn met with us in large groups before forming our small group that has been together for five years.

I love my writers group. We call it a writers group instead of a critique group, because we do far more than critique manuscripts. We also share information and gossip about publishers and agents, read reviews and rejection letters, carpool to events, and support each other during good times and bad. Through the years, three members had to go "back to work," but only Rita had to drop out entirely, and only because her work was in another part of the state. When we began we were six writers, one of whom had also owned a children's bookstore. Now there are nine of us. We all write, but we've added a retired librarian and two author/illustrators. We meet monthly, usually in the dining room of my home from 9:00 until after lunch, but we frequently talk on the phone or exchange e-mail between meetings. Like a child who believes she's in the best class in the school, I think I have the best writers group in the country. I am a professional writer, and the seven women and one man in my writers group are my valued colleagues.

While I never could have foreseen this five years ago, I also have online colleagues through the Writers Club on America Online. Most weekday mornings after Bill and the kids leave the house, I sit down at my computer to check my e-mail and the children's writers boards. Online bulletin boards are filled with an incredible amount of basic information for those just starting out writing for children. There is quite a bit of junk, too, but that's easily skipped. Authors with more than a hundred published books are willing to share expertise and encouragement. Editors and agents post messages as well. There are folders for frequently asked questions ("Can I mail a manuscript out to more than one publisher at the same time?") and ongoing discussions on both simple and esoteric aspects of being a children's writer. There's also a once-a-week chat (a virtual impossibility for me because it's at dinnertime in my time zone, but the text is easily downloaded). During the last national SCBWI conference I attended, several of us met in person for the first time and got together for meals. We still keep in touch through e-mail. There are also several Web sites especially for children's writers, and newsgroups as well.

I was interested to read the postings on AOL about the Institute of Children's Literature correspondence course. Several people wrote that it can be a great place to start: the materials are helpful, and the one-on-one instruction keeps writers on their toes. As with any class, people need to be willing to put sufficient time and effort — along with money — into it if they want to get much out of it. One of my AOL buddies, Karen, considers the ICL newsletter, *Children's Writer*, a gold mine of information, and also has good things to say about the contests they hold. Particularly for those who don't have access to workshops taught at community colleges or writing centers, ICL is worth investigating.

My favorite book about writing is not specifically about writing for children. Anne Lamott's witty, irreverent, and brilliant *Bird by Bird* has inspired me to sit down and write every day, thinking of myself as the "designated typist" as I tackle my assignments one chunk at a time ("bird by bird") and get that first draft down no matter how awful it is. I have two copies of *Bird by Bird* — a hardcover on the shelf in the office, and a paperback that I tuck in my bag if I think I might have to wait somewhere (and don't have children to read to).

Before I ever wrote a children's story, I carefully read several books about writing for children. Jane Yolen's *Guide to Writing for Children* and Barbara Seuling's *How to Write a Children's Book and Get it Published* were most helpful. I have also learned a great deal from three books of essays by esteemed children's authors: *The Seed and the Vision* by Eleanor Cameron; *Dreams and Wishes* by Susan Cooper; and *The Zena Sutherland Lectures*, a collection of speeches by distinguished writers and artists. I think of Anita Silvey's *Children's Books and their Creators* as a veritable encyclopedia of twentieth-century children's literature and a must-have resource for anyone who writes for children. For fun, I collect picture books by and about children's writers. Three I keep nearby are Daniel Pinkwater's *Author's Day; What Do Authors Do?* by Eileen Christelow; and Helen Lester's *Author: A True Story*. Each is funny and insightful. Finally, *The Annotated Charlotte's Web* is an incomparable teaching tool for how a classic children's book was crafted. I plan to reread it before I start writing another novel.

In addition to the *SCBWI Bulletin*, I subscribe to two other information-packed newsletters. *Once Upon a Time* is a folksy quarterly featuring inspirational and helpful short articles alongside columns by well-known writers and illustrators such as Barbara Seuling and Trina Schart Hyman. The monthly *Children's Book Insider* is more businesslike (it is edited by a former children's book editor), with articles that emphasize the basics of writing for the children's book and magazine market. It's useful for beginners and published authors alike. CBI also publishes how-to books that many writers swear by.

Long ago I made it a point to get to know my local children's librarian and bookseller. Field trips to the library and bookstore are vital to my work as a writer. What's new? What's great? What are people — publishers and parents — buying or checking out? What books are kids asking for? Even before I became an advocate as well as a writer of children's books, I read dozens of books every month.

Because I now also study review journals — especially *The Horn Book Magazine* and *Guide*, *School Library Journal*, *Publishers Weekly*, and *Book Links* — I sometimes hear about hot new books before my librarian and bookseller friends. I appreciate being able to help them, just as they continue to keep me informed. While I'll never write or draw like Peggy Rathmann or have the storytelling ability of Nancy Farmer, I can still learn from reading wonderful children's books. (A top children's book editor told those gathered at a national SCBWI conference about one of his authors once typing out an entire Judy Blume book, just to see how it was done.) I think it's important to read the Newbery and Caldecott winners and Honor books, and to get the list every year of ALA Notables from the American Library Association.

The market for selling a children's book manuscript has never been tighter. Medium-sized publishers are being swallowed up by big publishers, resulting in downsizing — fewer editors, fewer books. And yet ... writers who have creativity, talent, perseverance, professionalism, and stories to tell to young readers will always find a market. It isn't an easy business, and not many make a decent living even after publishing several books. But for those of us who feel we must write, it can be the most rewarding work imaginable — and possible, when we have spouses willing and able to support us.

A year (and a few crummy manuscripts) after I thought "I can do that," Rita and I drove up to San Francisco to walk around the exhibits at the annual meeting of the American Library Association. All the big publishers were there. We studied the new books on display, and listened to librarians chatting with editors about what they were looking for. At one booth, I overheard a librarian tell a publisher of special-needs books that she thought there was a market for a picture book for siblings of hospitalized children. I was so excited that I pulled Rita aside. "She's right!" I cried. "And I can write it, too."

Over the next week I turned Jennifer and Allison's experience into the first draft of what would become my first published picture book, *When Molly Was in the Hospital*. I ran it by my writers group several times through at least three drafts requested by the first publisher I sent it to (the same one I had overheard the librarian talking to at ALA). After a little over a year, the manuscript was returned "with regret" from the editor. Two weeks later I heard about Rayve Productions at a local SCBWI seminar, and within a week I had sold the manuscript. Determination, serendipity, and the willingness to revise had paid off. The book was illustrated and between covers a year later, and in June of 1995 it won a Benjamin Franklin Award at the annual meeting of the American Booksellers Association. We felt like we were at the Academy Awards! Even better, some children tell me it's their favorite book.

"Read and write, write and read," I advise anyone who asks how to become a children's book author. Join SCBWI, take a class, get a writers group together, subscribe to newsletters, hop on the Internet. Don't look for instant gratification, and be prepared for rejection. There are no shortcuts. My writing career has been a happy accident, but I've worked hard on it every day. And I never want to stop! ❦

Books

Cameron, Eleanor, *The Seed and the Vision: On the Writing and Appreciation of Children's Books* (1993)
Christelow, Eileen, *What Do Authors Do?* (1995)
Cooper, Susan, *Dreams and Wishes: Essays on Writing for Children* (1996)

Duncan, Debbie, *When Molly Was in the Hospital: A Book for Brothers and Sisters of Hospitalized Children*, illustrated by Nina Ollikainen, MD (1994)

Hearne, Betsy, editor, *The Zena Sutherland Lectures, 1983-1992* (1993)

Lamott, Anne, *Bird by Bird: Some Instructions on Writing and Life* (1994)

Lester, Helen, *Author: A True Story* (1997)

Neumeyer, Peter F., annotator, *The Annotated Charlotte's Web*, by E. B. White (1994)

Pinkwater, Daniel, *Author's Day* (1993)

Seuling, Barbara, *How to Write a Children's Book and Get it Published* (1984)

Silvey, Anita, editor, *Children's Books and Their Creators* (1995)

Yolen, Jane, *Guide to Writing for Children* (1989)

Organizations & Publications

Book Links
American Library Association
50 E. Huron St.
Chicago, IL 60611

Children's Book Insider
P.O. Box 1030
Fairplay, CO 80440-1030
http://www.write4kids.com

The Horn Book Magazine and *Guide*
The Horn Book, Inc.
11 Beacon Street
Boston, MA 02108

The Institute of Children's Literature
95 Long Ridge Rd.
West Redding, CT 55104

Once Upon a Time
553 Winston Court
St. Paul, MN 55118
http://members.aol.com/OUATMAG

Publishers Weekly
249 W. 17th St.
New York, NY 10011

SCBWI
22736 Vanowen Street, Suite 106
West Hills, CA 91037
http://www.scbwi.org

School Library Journal
245 W. 17th St.
New York, NY 10011

Web Sites

American Library Association
http://www.ala.org/

Children's Book Council
http://www.cbcbooks.org

Children's Literature Web Guide
http://www.ucalgary.ca/~dkbrown/index.html

Harold Underdown's Books for Children and More
http://www.users.interport.net/~hdu

The Slush Pile
http://www.theslushpile.com

America Online Writers Club (for AOL subscribers)
Keyword: Writers
Click on Messages, scroll to "Writers for Children/YA" for children's
    writers message boards

Final Thoughts

Twelve years ago I first went shopping for a book for my baby, knowing I wanted her to grow up loving books and reading. Call it a peculiar maternal instinct. I had a destination, but I lacked the proper road map. Where should I begin? Thanks to the good advice of a helpful and knowledgeable bookstore staffer, I started mapping my own route toward family literacy with a single book. The journey continues.

All three of my children find joy in reading. They were able to read independently by the middle of first grade. More important, though, they continue to look to books for entertainment and inspiration. Was this an accident? Probably not. Reading is a way of life in our home, as much as eating and teeth brushing are. It's a habit — one we all enjoy immensely. When Jennifer and Allison occasionally grumble that they can't turn a decent cartwheel, I tell them not to worry. "When you're thirty years old, no one will care if you ever learned to do a cartwheel." But reading — ah, that's a different story altogether. A child whose life is full of books will always have a friend and a conversation. Reading opens doors to the world (as well as college and careers).

Parents don't have to redirect their own careers to studying and writing children's books, as I have, in order to raise children who are friends with the written word. Read to your baby, your child, your adolescent. If you need inspiration, read *Better Than Life*, a marvelous book by a French author, Daniel Pennac, that makes the strongest case I have seen for reading to teens. He isn't the only one. Poet laureate Robert Pinsky believes passionately in reading aloud, and still reads aloud to his three daughters, who are between twenty and thirty years old.

I began by holding Jennifer in my lap in the red rocking chair and reading to her every night. We continue to connect over books. Now, instead of the rocking chair, we sit at the kitchen table late at night and talk over angel food cake. We read together whenever possible. She's developed her own tastes in literature, as have her sisters. They all have their favorite authors and books. We discuss and rate them at the dinner table. We're learning from each other all the time.

Over the last dozen years, I have read thousands of children's books and hundreds of articles and books on children's literacy. I do have some final thoughts and nuts-and-bolts advice for parents on ways to nourish a love of books and reading:

• Set a good example and read. Children, especially young children, learn from watching their parents. Kids should see Mom and Dad reading for pleasure.

• Establish a routine of daily family reading for a minimum of fifteen to twenty minutes, and work up from there. Begin by reading aloud to your little one, and continue reading even as your child is able to read to himself. His "listening level" is higher than his reading level, and reading aloud more challenging books will help increase vocabulary and sharpen critical thinking skills.

• Read with expression. "Be a ham," advises writer and National Public Radio commentator Daniel Pinkwater. (Bill agrees.)

♦ Have "theme nights" for your read-alouds — bears, vacations, summer, grandparents, blankets, dogs, whatever — and ask your preschooler if she can guess what the theme is.

♦ Take time to listen to your child read aloud. It's fun, and you'll also be able to spot any problems he may be having reading. If that's the case, your next step may be to get help from the school.

♦ Invite older children to read to their younger brothers or sisters. It's good for all age groups. We sometimes pass a book up and down the couch so everyone can read a page.

♦ Encourage your child to write, for reading and writing are inextricably linked.

♦ Save toddler books for easy readers.

♦ Read aloud at different times of the day, not just before bed. Reading can dispel the boredom of a rainy afternoon or calm a hurt or angry child.

♦ Don't panic if you fall out of the read-aloud habit with older kids. They get busier as they get older, and if you have younger children, you're spending your evenings reading with them. (My friend Catherine had her two kids less than two years apart. It was rough when Leah and Josh were babies, but for the last several years they've been able to share the same books read aloud. In our family, five-and-a-half years separate Jennifer and Molly. Rarely do we find a chapter book that's right for both of them.) If days, weeks, or even months go by without reading aloud, just pick a book you think both of you will enjoy and begin again.

♦ For older kids, stop at the cliffhanger, usually the end of a chapter. It will leave your child eager for the next day's installment. (There are some books, I know, that simply must be finished — bedtime or no bedtime.)

♦ Save holiday books to bring out every year.

♦ Control television time. Make reading the preferred activity.

♦ Make independent reading a habit. Studies have shown that children who read at least one book a week for six months significantly improve their reading ability. Children become good readers by . . . (drumroll, please) READING.

• Get a clip-on book light so your older child can read easily in bed without disturbing younger roommates. It works better than a flashlight. Jennifer now has her own bedroom, but she likes using the book light anyway because she doesn't have to get out of bed to turn off the light.

• Have books and other reading and writing materials all over your home. Make it easier to pick up a book than the TV remote control. Take books with you when your child has a doctor's appointment. Save special books for family vacations. Herbert Hoover wanted "a chicken in every pot." I'd campaign on the pledge: "a bookshelf in every room," *especially* every child's room. It doesn't need to be fancy or filled with expensive hardcovers, it simply should be a place for your child to collect her own books. Look for them at yard sales or secondhand bookstores. If you have a good location in your home, consider investing in one of those magazine-style bookshelves. Classrooms use them because they make the books so accessible: they're right there, face-forward, you can't miss 'em.

• Take advantage of mail-order book clubs such as Book-of-the-Month Club and Junior Library Guild, especially if you're busy and you'd like to have an expert *do* the culling for you. I know parents who have discovered some of their families' favorite books this way.

• Also, study those school book order forms when they come home. The books are inexpensive, and kids love to make their own selections. They're ownable, theirs. "Book orders are here!" kids shout when the big box arrives in the classroom. We first met Marc Brown's Arthur character through book orders, as well as Rosemary Wells's hilarious *Max's Dragon Shirt* and Nancy Carlson's rip-roaring ride, *Harriet and the Roller Coaster.* What finds! If your child's teacher doesn't use book clubs, ask if time is keeping her from organizing it. Then offer to do it yourself. It's not hard, and it's a wonderful way to help out at the school (classrooms earn free books).

I make a lousy room parent (all those parties), or classroom volunteer (I'm not as patient with other people's children), but I can organize book orders in a few hours at home on a weekend. Anyone can.

◆ Ask for books or magazine subscriptions for birthday and holiday presents, and give them yourself. I never had to ask, but my dear college friend Marilyn always sent books for my daughters' birthdays. *Dogger*, *If You Give a Mouse a Cookie*, and *Chicka Chicka Boom Boom* have certainly outlasted any toys my girls received when they were little. By a mile.

◆ Magazines: We like *Ladybug* and *Spider* a lot. We discovered our favorite Tomie dePaola book, *Haircuts for the Woolseys*, in *Ladybug*. I remember when Jennifer eagerly awaited the arrival of *Spider* in our mailbox so she could read the next installment of Ursula K. Le Guin's *Catwings*. *American Girl* is another magazine we've subscribed to since its premier issue. Some families swear by *Highlights*, *Cobblestone*, *Owl*, or *Ranger Rick*. Others like *Sports Illustrated for Kids*. One five-year-old boy I know loves *National Geographic*. Whatever your child's interest, capitalize on it.

◆ If you've read everything in my book so far, you know how I feel about the library. Use it. Make sure your children know how to use it. Get them library cards. Make friends with the children's librarian. Look for recent acquisitions on the new books shelf. Follow up on favorite author finds by checking out more books by that author. It's free!

◆ Look for award-winning children's books — Caldecotts, Newberys, Coretta Scott Kings, and state award nominees. The American Library Association lists Notable books on the ALA Web site. With up to five thousand children's books published annually, it's nice to know what librarians and teachers consider the best books of the year. Go back and read winners from previous years, too. There is a wonderful ALA paperback publication, *The Newbery and Caldecott Awards*, published annually, that lists and describes all the winners, including Honor books. Did you know, for example, that

Charlotte's Web was a Newbery Honor book the year *Secret of the Andes* (huh?) won the Medal? Be on the lookout for award-winning authors who are on book-signing tours. We have autographed copies of the 1996 Newbery and Caldecott Award winners, *The Midwife's Apprentice* and *Officer Buckle and Gloria*, among the stars on our shelves.

◆ Check out the ALA Web site, too, for the location of the annual ALA conference. It takes place at the end of June/beginning of July, and if it is within one hundred miles of your home — GO! Take your children. You needn't be a librarian to attend the biggest show of children's books. For a small fee, you can get a pass to the exhibits and have the time of your lives seeing the new books, meeting the people who create them, and loading up on award-winning titles. I took Jennifer and Allison to the 1997 ALA conference in San Francisco, where they were able to ask Avi what his last name was. (Avi didn't answer the question, but he talked with the girls and signed a free copy of *The True Confessions of Charlotte Doyle*, a book Jennifer adores.) Allison told Rosemary Wells what her favorite "Bunny Planet" book is. ("Thank you, Allison," replied one of our favorite authors warmly.) We all saw what E. L. Konigsburg looks like. (She had won the Newbery for *The View from Saturday*, so her line was too long for an autograph.) Jennifer just missed meeting Francesca Lia Block, but Allison let Emily Arnold McCully know that she likes to read her books from our easy reader bookshelf. ("You have an easy reader bookshelf in your home?" the kind author and illustrator asked my child as she signed *Grandmas at the Lake* for Molly.) We managed to run into Nancy Farmer and Peggy Rathmann in the aisles. After all this, Allison decided she wanted to go to ALA every year. "It'll be back in San Francisco in five years," I said as we lugged our bags of books out the convention-center doors. "We'll go again then."

◆ Donating old books to Goodwill, or perhaps a children's hospital or shelter, is a good way to keep books in circulation that your kids may have outgrown. Save the favorites, however, for your children to start their own libraries when they become parents.

• Audio books make great entertainment on long car trips. We listened to *Anne of Green Gables* on the way to Lake Tahoe one year (until the driver, Bill, said it was putting him to sleep). Allison occasionally still plays the tape before bed. One mother says that her (now) teenage son has always learned best by listening; he has heard every audio book in our public library, and they bought the tapes he liked best to listen to at home.

• Books on CD-ROM are fine, although expensive, toys. Molly was three when we first got *Arthur's Teacher Trouble* on CD-ROM. She was fascinated by the power she had in her little hand — things *happened* to the book on the screen when she clicked the mouse! I give the program credit for helping my little one become comfortable with the computer. But it didn't replace the book which she could hold in her hands and snuggle up with next to me on the couch or take to bed with her at night.

• Share books and reading. Talk about books at dinner-time. Borrow expressions and characters from favorite books and make them part of your family culture. Encourage your kids to share books with friends. Jennifer and two of her classmates read the first couple of chapters of *A Girl Named Disaster* to each other over the telephone when they were assigned to read it for school, until the book became so engrossing that each girl finished it on her own within a few days. My friend Karen has fond memories of shared reading in elementary school, of handing a book to someone and asking every now and then, "What part are you up to?" When the friend laughed, Karen would ask what it was about, and then they'd both laugh together. How wonderful! I do that now with Jennifer and Allison. I practically looked over their shoulders the entire time they were reading *Frindle*.

Books have the power to touch our hearts and bring us together. They teach us about the world and ourselves. They give us uncommon joy. Reading is the key to it all.

Books

Avi, *The True Confessions of Charlotte Doyle* (1990)

Carlson, Nancy, *Harriet and the Roller Coaster* (1982)

Clark, Ann Nolan, *Secret of the Andes*, illustrated by Jean Charlot (1952)

Clements, Andrew, *Frindle*, illustrated by Brian Selznick (1996)

Cushman, Karen, *The Midwife's Apprentice* (1995)

dePaola, Tomie, *Haircuts for the Woolseys* (1989)

Farmer, Nancy, *A Girl Named Disaster* (1996)

Hughes, Shirley, *Dogger* (1988)

Konigsburg, E. L., *The View from Saturday* (1996)

LeGuin, Ursula K., "Catwings," *Spider* Premier Issue (January 1994)

Martin, Bill, Jr. and John Archambault, *Chicka Chicka Boom Boom*, illustrated by Lois Ehlert (1989)

McCully, Emily Arnold, *Grandmas at the Lake* (1990)

Numeroff, Laura Joffe, *If You Give a Mouse a Cookie*, illustrated by Felicia Bond (1985)

Pennac, Daniel, *Better Than Life*, translated by David Homel (1994)

Rathmann, Peggy, *Officer Buckle and Gloria* (1995)

Wells, Rosemary, *Max's Dragon Shirt* (1991)

White, E. B., *Charlotte's Web*, illustrated by Garth Williams (1952)

The Newbery and Caldecott Awards: A Guide to the Medal and Honor Books (published annually by the Association of Library Service to Children, American Library Association)

Magazines

American Girl
Pleasant Company Publications
8400 Fairway Place
Middleton, WI 53562

Babybug, Ladybug, Spider, Cricket
Carus Publishing Company
P.O. Box 300
Peru, IL 61354

Cobblestone, The History Magazine for Young People
Cobblestone Publishing, Inc.
7 School St.
Peterborough, NH 03458

Highlights for Children
803 Church St.
Honesdale, PA 18431

National Geographic
National Geographic Society
1145 17th St. NW
Washington, DC 20036

Owl Magazine, The Discovery Magazine for Children
179 John St., Suite 50
Toronto, Ontario
M5T 3G5
Canada

Ranger Rick
National Wildlife Federation
8925 Leesburg Pike
Vienna, VA 22184

Sports Illustrated for Kids
Time & Life Building
New York, NY 10020

And . . .

Web site for the American Library Association
http://www.ala.org/

101 Favorite Books

These children's books, and the order in which they appear (roughly by age of the audience, from babies through teens), inspired lively discussions around the kitchen counter in our home the weekend before *Joy of Reading* went to press. Choices were debated, counted ("Can't we have 102, Mom?"), ordered, and reordered. There wasn't one hundred percent agreement on every title. Yet that is as it should be, because not everyone has precisely the same taste in literature, even within the same family. We offer this list as a beginning — for a home library, or perhaps for books to seek out at the public library. There is, after all, no real end to a listing of a family's favorite books.

Good Night, Gorilla, Peggy Rathmann
Goodnight Moon, Margaret Wise Brown, illustrated by Clement Hurd
Owl Babies, Martin Waddell, illustrated by Patrick Benson
Corduroy, Don Freeman
Caps for Sale, Esphyr Slobodkina
The Snowy Day, Ezra Jack Keats
Guess How Much I Love You, Sam McBratney, illustrated by Anita Jeram
Brown Bear, Brown Bear, What Do You See?, Bill Martin, Jr., illustrated by Eric Carle
The Very Hungry Caterpillar, Eric Carle

Madeline, Ludwig Bemelmans

Voyage to the Bunny Planet, Rosemary Wells

Jesse Bear, What Will You Wear?, Nancy White Carlstrom, illustrated by Bruce Degen

Somebody and the Three Blairs, Marilyn Tolhurst, illustrated by Simone Abel

Sylvester and the Magic Pebble, William Steig

Ira Sleeps Over, Bernard Waber

Alexander and the Terrible, Horrible, No Good, Very Bad Day, Judith Viorst, illustrated by Ray Cruz

Martha Speaks, Susan Meddaugh

Martha Blah Blah, Susan Meddaugh

Arthur's Family Vacation, Marc Brown

Blueberries for Sal, Robert McCloskey

Chicka Chicka Boom Boom, Bill Martin, Jr. and John Archambault, illustrated by Lois Ehlert

Where the Wild Things Are, Maurice Sendak

The Relatives Came, Cynthia Rylant, illustrated by Stephen Gammell

Julius, the Baby of the World, Kevin Henkes

Chrysanthemum, Kevin Henkes

If You Give a Mouse a Cookie, Laura Joffe Numeroff, illustrated by Felicia Bond

When Bluebell Sang, Lisa Campbell Ernst

Dogger, Shirley Hughes

The Cow Who Wouldn't Come Down, Paul Brett Johnson

Harry and Tuck, Holly Keller

Officer Buckle and Gloria, Peggy Rathmann

Ruby the Copycat, Peggy Rathmann

Annabelle Swift, Kindergartner, Amy Schwartz

Flat Stanley, Jeff Brown, illustrated by Tomi Ungerer

The Polar Express, Chris Van Allsburg

The Cat in the Hat, Dr. Seuss

Hop on Pop, Dr. Seuss

Amelia Bedelia, Peggy Parish, illustrated by Fritz Siebel

The Blue Hill Meadows, Cynthia Rylant, illustrated by Ellen Beier

The True Story of the 3 Little Pigs, Jon Scieszka, illustrated by Lane Smith

The Stinky Cheese Man and Other Fairly Stupid Tales, Jon Scieszka, illustrated by Lane Smith

"Never Spit on Your Shoes," Denys Cazet

"Are There Any Questions?," Denys Cazet

Amber Brown Is Not a Crayon, Paula Danziger, illustrated by Tony Ross
Charlotte's Web, E. B. White, illustrated by Garth Williams
Frindle, Andrew Clements, illustrated by Brian Selznick
All About Sam, Lois Lowry, illustrated by Diane deGroat
The Boggart, Susan Cooper
Homer Price, Robert McCloskey
The Wonderful Flight to the Mushroom Planet, Eleanor Cameron
Ribsy, Beverly Cleary, illustrated by Louis Darling
Ramona and Her Father, Beverly Cleary, illustrated by Alan Tiegreen
The Moffats, Eleanor Estes
Winnie-the-Pooh, A. A. Milne, illustrated by Ernest Shepard
The House at Pooh Corner, A. A. Milne, illustrated by Ernest Shepard
Ace: The Very Important Pig, Dick King-Smith, illustrated by Lynette
    Hernmant
Do You Know Me, Nancy Farmer, illustrated by Shelley Jackson
Sarah, Plain and Tall, Patricia MacLachlan
Amelia's Notebook, Marissa Moss
Maybe Yes, Maybe No, Maybe Maybe, Susan Patron, illustrated
    by Dorothy Donahue
Ginger Pye, Eleanor Estes
Half Magic, Edward Eager
The Phantom Tollbooth, Norton Juster, illustrated by Jules Feiffer
The BFG, Roald Dahl, illustrated by Quentin Blake
The Witches, Roald Dahl, illustrated by Quentin Blake
Time for Andrew: A Ghost Story, Mary Downing Hahn
Brooklyn Doesn't Rhyme, Joan W. Blos
The Best School Year Ever, Barbara Robinson
Joyful Noise: Poems for Two Voices, Paul Fleischman, illustrated by
    Eric Beddows
The Lion, the Witch and the Wardrobe, C. S. Lewis
Harriet the Spy, Louise Fitzhugh
Dear Mr. Henshaw, Beverly Cleary, illustrated by Paul O. Zelinsky
Number the Stars, Lois Lowry
The Exiles, Hilary McKay
The Indian in the Cupboard, Lynne Reid Banks, illustrated by Brock Cole
In the Year of the Boar and Jackie Robinson, Bette Bao Lord,
    illustrated by Marc Simont
The Witch of Blackbird Pond, Elizabeth George Speare
Baby, Patricia MacLachlan
Tuck Everlasting, Natalie Babbitt
Freak the Mighty, Rodman Philbrick

From the Mixed-Up Files of Mrs. Basil E. Frankweiler, E. L. Konigsburg
Seedfolks, Paul Fleischman, illustrated by Judy Pedersen
The Ear, the Eye and the Arm, Nancy Farmer
M. C. Higgins, the Great, Virginia Hamilton
A Wrinkle in Time, Madeleine L'Engle
Bridge to Terabithia, Katherine Paterson
Anne of Green Gables, L. M. Montgomery
Hatchet, Gary Paulsen
Anastasia at This Address, Lois Lowry
The Watsons Go to Birmingham — 1963, Christopher Paul Curtis
The Glory Field, Walter Myers
The Giver, Lois Lowry
A Girl Named Disaster, Nancy Farmer
The Golden Compass, Philip Pullman
I Am an Artichoke, Lucy Frank
The Ruby in the Smoke, Philip Pullman
Weetzie Bat, Francesca Lia Block
A Fate Totally Worse than Death, Paul Fleischman
Make Lemonade, Virginia Euwer Wolff
Staying Fat for Sarah Byrnes, Chris Crutcher
Girl Goddess #9: Nine Stories, Francesca Lia Block

Afterward

Joy of Reading lives on! I will continue to read and write about children's books and I want to hear from you, the reader, about your family's favorite books. Please visit my Web site at www.debbieduncan.com to find out what Jennifer, Allison, Molly, and I are reading and what new books we like, link to some of my favorite Web sites, and send me e-mail. You may also write to me the old-fashioned way at Rayve Productions Inc., P.O. Box 726, Windsor, CA 95492.

Index

Two indexes follow: a listing of children's books by title, and a listing of children's books authors and illustrators.

Title Index

Author & Illustrator Index

ABOUT RAYVE PRODUCTIONS

Rayve Productions is an award-winning small publisher of books and music. Current publications are primarily in the following categories:

(1) Business guidebooks for home-based businesses and other entrepreneurs
(2) Quality children's books and music
(3) History books about America and her regions, and an heirloom-quality journal for creating personal histories.

Rayve Productions' mail-order catalog offers the above items plus business books, software, music, and other enjoyable items produced by others.

Our eclectic collection of business resources and gift items has something to please everyone.

A FREE catalog is available upon request.

Come visit us at www.spannet.org/rayve.

CHILDREN'S BOOKS & MUSIC

☆ *Link Across America: A story of the historic Lincoln Highway*
by Mary Elizabeth Anderson
ISBN 1-877810-97-5, hardcover, $14.95, 1997 pub.
It began with a long-ago dream . . . a road that would run clear across America! The dream became reality in 1914 as the Lincoln Highway began to take form, to eventually run from New York City to San Francisco. Venture from past to present experiencing transportation history. Topics include Abraham Lincoln, teams of horses, seedling miles, small towns, making concrete, auto courts, Burma Shave signs, classic cars and road rallies. Color photos along today's Lincoln Highway remnants, b/w historical photos, map and list of cities along the old Lincoln Highway. (Ages 7-13 & their parents, grandparents & great-grandparents)

☆ *The Perfect Orange: A tale from Ethiopia*
by Frank P. Araujo, PhD; illustrated by Xiao Jun Li
ISBN 1-877810-94-0, hardcover, $16.95, 1994 pub., Toucan Tales volume 2
Inspiring gentle folktale. Breathtaking watercolors dramatize ancient Ethiopia's contrasting pastoral charm and majesty. Illustrations are rich with Ethiopian details. Story reinforces values of generosity and selflessness over greed and self-centeredness. Glossary of Ethiopian terms and pronunciation key.
(**PBS** *Storytime* **Selection**; Recommended by *School Library Journal, Faces, MultiCultural Review, Small Press Magazine, The Five Owls, Wilson Library Bulletin*)

☆ *Nekane, the Lamiña & the Bear: A tale of the Basque Pyrenees*
by Frank P. Araujo, PhD; illustrated by Xiao Jun Li
ISBN 1-877810-01-0, hardcover, $16.95, 1993 pub., Toucan Tales volume 1
Delightful Basque folktale pits appealing, quick-witted young heroine against mysterious villain. Lively, imaginative narrative, sprinkled with Basque phrases. Vibrant watercolor images. Glossary of Basque terms and pronunciation key.
(Recommended by School Library Journal, Publishers Weekly, Kirkus Reviews, Booklist, Wilson Library Bulletin, The Basque Studies Program Newsletter: University of Nevada, BCCB, The Five Owls)

☆ *The Laughing River: A folktale for peace*
by Elizabeth Haze Vega; illustrated by Ashley Smith, 1995 pub.
ISBN 1-877810-35-5   hardcover book, $16.95
ISBN 1-877810-36-3   companion musical audiotape, $9.95
ISBN 1-877810-37-1   book & musical audiotape combo, $23.95
Drum kit, $9.95
Book, musical audiotape & drum kit combo, $29.95
Two fanciful African tribes are in conflict until the laughing river bubbles melodiously into their lives, bringing fun, friendship, peace. Lyrical fanciful folktale of conflict resolution. Mesmerizing music. Dancing, singing and drumming instructions. Orff approach. (Recommended by *School Library Journal*)

☆ *When Molly Was in the Hospital: A book for brothers and sisters of hospitalized children*

by Debbie Duncan; illustrated by Nina Ollikainen, MD

ISBN 1-877810-44-4, hardcover, $12.95, 1994 pub.

Anna's little sister, Molly, has been very ill and had to have an operation. Anna tells us all about the experience from her point of view. Sensitive, insightful, heartwarming story. A support and comfort for siblings and those who love them. Authentic. Realistic. Effective.

(Winner of 1995 Benjamin Franklin Award: Best Children's Picture Book. Recommended by *Children's Book Insider, School Library Journal, Disabilities Resources Monthly*)

☆ *Night Sounds*

by Lois G. Grambling; illustrated by Randall F. Ray

ISBN 1-877810-77-0, hardcover, $12.95   ISBN 1-877810-83-5, softcover, $6.95, 1996 pub.

Perfect bedtime story. Ever so gently, a child's thoughts slip farther and farther away, moving from purring cat at bedside and comical creatures in the yard to distant trains and church bells, and then at last, to sleep. Imaginative, lilting text and daringly unpretentious b/w watercolor illustrations

☆ *Los Sonidos de la Noche*

by Lois G. Grambling; illustrated by Randall F. Ray

(Spanish edition of *Night Sounds*), 1996 pub.

ISBN 1-877810-76-2, hardcover, $12.95   ISBN 1-877810-82-7, softcover, $6.95

BUSINESS & CAREER

☆ *Smart Tax Write-offs: Hundreds of tax deduction ideas for home-based businesses, independent contractors, all entrepreneurs*
by Norm Ray, CPA
ISBN 1-877810-20-7, softcover, $12.95, 1996 pub.
Fun-to-read, easy-to-use guidebook that encourages entrepreneurs to be aggressive and creative in taking legitimate tax deductions. Includes valuable checklist of over 600 write-off ideas. Every small business owner's "must read." (Recommended by *Home Office Computing, Small Business Opportunities, Spare Time, Independent Business Magazine*).

☆ *The Independent Medical Transcriptionist, 3rd edition: The comprehensive guidebook for career success in a home-based medical transcription business* by Donna Avila-Weil, CMT and Mary Glaccum, CMT
ISBN 1-877810-23-1, softcover, $34.95, 1997 pub.
The industry's premier reference book for medical transcription entrepreneurs. (Recommended by *Journal of the American Association for Medical Transcription, Entrepreneur, Small Business Opportunities*)

☆ *Independent Medical Coding: The comprehensive guidebook for career success as a home-based medical coder*
by Donna Avila-Weil, CMT and Rhonda Regan, CCS
ISBN 1-877810-17-7, softcover, $34.95, 1997 pub.
How to start and successfully run your own professional independent medical coding business. Step-by-step instructions.

☆ *Easy Financials for Your Home-based Business*   by Norm Ray, CPA
ISBN 1-877810-92-4, softcover, $19.95, 1992 pub.
Small business & home-based business expert helps you save time by making your work easier, and save money by nailing down your tax deductions. (Recommended by *Wilson Library Bulletin, The Business Journal, National Home Business Report*)

☆ *Internal Medicine Words*   by Minta Danna
ISBN 1-877810-68-1, softcover, $29.95, 1997 pub.
Over 8,000 words and terms related to internal medicine. A valuable spelling and terminology usage resource for medical transcriptionists, medical writers and editors, court reporters, medical records personnel, and others working with medical documentation.

☆ *Shrinking the Globe into Your Company's Hands: The step-by-step international trade guide for small businesses*   by Sidney R. Lawrence, PE
ISBN 1-877810-46-0, softcover, $24.95, 1997 pub.
An expert in foreign trade shows U.S. small business owners how to market and export products and services safely and profitably.

HISTORY

☆ *20 Tales of California: A rare collection of western stories*   by Hector Lee
ISBN 1-877810-63-0, hardcover, $16.95
ISBN 1-877810-62-2, softcover, $9.95, 1997 pub.
Mysterious and romantic tales: real life and folklore set in various California locations. Includes ideas for family outings and classroom field trips.

☆ *Link Across America: A story of the historic Lincoln Highway* — see Children's Books

☆ *Windsor, The Birth of a City*   by Gabriel A. Fraire
ISBN 1-877810-91-6, hardcover, $21.95, 1991 pub.
Fascinating case study of political and social issues surrounding city incorporation of Windsor, California, 1978—1991. LAFCO impact.

☆ *LifeTimes, The Life Experiences Journal*
ISBN 1-877810-34-7, hardcover, $49.95
World's easiest, most fun and useful personal journal. Handsome heirloom quality with gilt-edged pages. Over 150 information categories to record your life experiences. Winner of national award for excellence.

GENERAL

☆ *Nancy's Candy Cookbook: How to make candy at home the easy way*
by Nancy Shipman
ISBN 1-877810-65-7, softcover, $14.95, 1996 pub.
Have fun and save money by making candy at home at a fraction of candy store prices. More than 100 excellent candy recipes — from Grandma's delicious old-fashioned fudge to modern gourmet truffles. Includes many children's favorites, too.

☆ *Joy of Reading: One family's fun-filled guide to reading success*
by Debbie Duncan
ISBN 1-877810-45-2, softcover, $14.95, 1998 pub.
A dynamic author and mother, and an expert on children's literature, shares her family's personal reading success stories. You'll be inspired and entertained by this lighthearted, candid glimpse into one family's daily experiences as they cope with the ups and downs of life. Through it all, there is love, and an abundance of wonderful books to mark the milestones along the way.

ORDER

For mail orders please complete this order form and forward with check, money order or credit card information to Rayve Productions, POB 726, Windsor CA 95492. If paying with a credit card, you can call us toll-free at **800.852.4890** or fax this completed form to Rayve Productions at 707.838.2220.

You can also order at our web site at www.spannet.org/rayve.

☐ Please send me the following book(s):

Title _____ Price _____ Qty _____Amount _____

Title _____ Price _____ Qty _____Amount _____

Title _____ Price _____ Qty _____Amount _____

Title _____ Price _____ Qty _____Amount _____

Total Amount _____

Sales Tax: Californians please add 7.5% sales tax　　　Sales Tax _____

S/H: Book rate --- $3 for first book + $.50 each additional　　Shipping _____
　　　Priority --- $4 for first book + $.75 each additional

Total _____

Name _____ Phone _____

Address _____

City State Zip _____

☐ Check enclosed $ _____ Date _____

☐ Charge my Visa/MC/Discover/AMEX $_____

Credit card # _____ Exp. _____

Signature _____ *Thank you!*